THE HIDDEN FORCES WITHIN

Understanding the Psychology Behind Action

Table of Contents

Introduction

Human beings like to believe they are the authors of their own actions. We tell ourselves that we act because we choose to, because we want to, or because logic and reason guide our decisions. Yet when we look closely at how people actually behave—what they repeat, what they avoid, what they pursue against their own better judgment—a different picture begins to emerge. Much of human action is not as deliberate as it appears. Beneath every visible behavior lies a network of hidden psychological forces quietly shaping direction, momentum, and outcome.

The Hidden Forces Within explores these forces.

Every day, people promise change and then return to old patterns. They plan carefully and still sabotage themselves. They know what is good for them, yet act otherwise. This contradiction is not a failure of intelligence or morality—it is a function of psychology. Action is rarely driven by conscious thought alone. It is the product of habits, emotions, beliefs, perceptions, identity, and social conditioning operating largely outside of awareness.

This book begins with a simple but powerful premise: **to understand action, we must understand the mind beneath it**.

Psychology is often discussed in abstract terms—concepts, theories, diagnoses—but its true significance lies in how it translates into behavior. Why does one person persist while another quits? Why do some individuals act decisively while others remain trapped in hesitation? Why do people repeat destructive behaviors even when the consequences are clear? These questions cannot be answered by motivation alone. They require a deeper examination of the mental systems that drive action long before choice enters the picture.

At the core of human behavior is an invisible architecture. This architecture is built over time through experience, repetition, emotional conditioning, and social influence. Once established, it operates automatically, conserving mental energy by guiding behavior without constant conscious input. This efficiency is useful—but it can also be limiting. When outdated patterns remain unexamined, they quietly dictate actions that no longer serve the individual.

One of the most misunderstood aspects of human psychology is the relationship between intention and behavior. Intention feels powerful because it is conscious, verbal, and emotionally charged. Yet intention alone often fails to produce lasting change. This is why motivation surges fade, why resolutions dissolve, and why insight does not automatically lead to transformation. Action follows the strongest psychological force in the moment—not the most logical one.

That force may be emotion, habit, fear, identity, or social pressure.

Emotions, for example, are not merely reactions; they are engines of movement. Fear can immobilize or accelerate. Pleasure can reinforce repetition. Anxiety can narrow perception and distort decision-making. Over time, emotional experiences become encoded into memory, linking certain feelings to specific behaviors. Once established, these emotional-action loops activate automatically, often bypassing rational evaluation.

Similarly, habits are not just repeated behaviors; they are neurological shortcuts. The brain, designed for efficiency, prefers patterns it has already learned. When a behavior has been repeated often enough, it becomes the default response, activated with little conscious effort. This is why change feels difficult—not because people lack willpower, but because they are working against deeply ingrained mental pathways.

Beliefs add another layer to this system. What a person believes about themselves, the world, and their capabilities quietly shapes what actions feel possible or impossible. A belief does not need to be true to be powerful; it only needs to be accepted. Once internalized, beliefs act as filters, determining which options are considered and which are dismissed without examination.

Perception further complicates this process. Human beings do not respond to reality as it is; they respond to reality as it is interpreted. Two individuals can face the same situation and act in completely different ways because their minds construct different meanings from the same information. These interpretations are influenced by past experiences, emotional states, cognitive biases, and social conditioning.

Social forces are equally influential. From early childhood, behavior is shaped through approval, rejection, reward, and punishment. Cultural norms define what is acceptable. Authority figures influence compliance. Group identity reinforces conformity. Over time, external expectations become internalized, guiding behavior even in the absence of direct pressure. Many actions that feel personal are, in fact, socially conditioned responses.

At the center of all these forces lies identity—the story people tell themselves about who they are. Identity is not static; it is reinforced through action and, in turn, reinforces future behavior. People tend to act in ways that are consistent with their self-image, even when that image is limiting. Change often fails not because new behaviors are impossible, but because they conflict with an existing identity.

This book does not treat human behavior as random or irrational. On the contrary, it assumes that all behavior is logical when viewed from the perspective of the psychological system that produces it. Even self-sabotage serves a function—often protection, familiarity, or emotional regulation. By understanding the function, individuals gain the power to interrupt automatic patterns and choose differently.

The Hidden Forces Within is not about quick fixes or surface-level motivation. It is about awareness. Awareness of how actions are formed, why they repeat, and what sustains them. Awareness creates distance between impulse and response. In that space, intentional action becomes possible.

Throughout this book, you will be guided through the unseen mechanisms that shape behavior—from motivation and habit to emotion, belief, identity, and self-regulation. Each chapter builds toward a deeper understanding of how action emerges and how it can be redesigned from the inside out.

True freedom is not the absence of influence—it is the ability to recognize influence and respond consciously. When the hidden forces within are brought into awareness, action no longer feels mysterious or uncontrollable. It becomes something that can be understood, directed, and aligned with purpose.

This is the journey this book invites you to take: not toward perfection, but toward clarity. Not toward control, but toward conscious choice. And ultimately, toward action that reflects not habit or conditioning—but intention.

Chapter 1

The Architecture of Human Action

Human action appears simple on the surface. A thought arises, a decision is made, and behavior follows. This linear explanation is comforting, but it is incomplete. In reality, action emerges from a layered psychological structure in which conscious intention is only one component—and often not the most influential. To understand why people act as they do, it is necessary to examine the underlying architecture that governs behavior long before choice feels deliberate.

This chapter introduces the foundational idea that human action is driven by both conscious and unconscious forces working simultaneously. While conscious thought provides reasoning, justification, and narrative, unconscious processes supply speed, efficiency, and emotional weight. The unconscious mind continuously evaluates information, drawing on past experiences, emotional memory, and learned patterns to guide behavior without requiring active awareness. By the time a person believes they have "decided," much of the psychological work has already been completed.

Within this architecture lie psychological triggers—internal and external cues that activate specific responses. These triggers can be emotional states, environmental signals, social interactions, or internal beliefs. Often, individuals are unaware of what has triggered their behavior, yet they experience the action as self-chosen. This disconnect explains why certain behaviors repeat despite conscious efforts to change them.

Decision-making, therefore, is not a single moment but a process that unfolds beneath awareness. The mind weighs perceived threats, rewards, and familiarity before conscious reasoning enters the picture. What feels like free choice is frequently the final step in a chain of automatic evaluations designed to conserve energy and maintain psychological stability.

By exploring the architecture of human action, this chapter lays the groundwork for understanding behavior as a system rather than a series of isolated choices. Once this structure is recognized, patterns that once seemed irrational begin to make sense—and meaningful change becomes possible.

Conscious vs. Unconscious Drivers

Human behavior is often explained as the result of conscious choice. People believe they act because they have decided to act, because they have evaluated options, weighed consequences, and selected a course of action. This belief reinforces a sense of control and personal responsibility. However, psychological research and everyday observation reveal a more complex reality. Conscious thought plays a role in behavior, but it is not the primary driver in most actions. Instead, behavior emerges from an ongoing interaction between conscious awareness and unconscious processes, with the latter exerting a far greater influence than is commonly acknowledged.

The conscious mind is responsible for deliberate thinking, reflection, planning, and self-explanation. It allows individuals to articulate reasons for their actions and to imagine future outcomes. When a person sets a goal, makes a promise, or forms an intention, these activities occur at the conscious level. Conscious thought also enables moral reasoning, long-term planning, and abstract problem-solving. Yet it operates slowly and requires effort. Because of its limited capacity, the conscious mind cannot manage the vast amount of information encountered every moment.

To compensate, the mind relies heavily on unconscious systems. The unconscious mind processes information rapidly, automatically, and continuously. It evaluates emotional significance, detects patterns, and initiates responses without requiring conscious attention. This system evolved to ensure survival, prioritizing speed and efficiency over accuracy or reflection. When a person instinctively withdraws from danger, feels uneasy around someone without knowing why, or reacts emotionally before thinking, unconscious processes are at work.

Most daily behaviors are guided by these unconscious drivers. Habits, routines, emotional reactions, and learned responses operate below awareness, allowing individuals to function without constant deliberation. While this automation is beneficial, it also explains why people often act in ways that contradict their stated intentions. A person may consciously want to change a behavior, yet repeatedly fail because unconscious patterns remain intact. The conscious desire for change is simply not strong enough to override deeply embedded automatic responses.

One of the key differences between conscious and unconscious drivers lies in how they handle information. The conscious mind evaluates choices using logic and language, while the unconscious mind relies on associations, emotional memory, and prior experience. When faced with a situation, the unconscious quickly categorizes it as familiar or unfamiliar, safe or threatening, rewarding or risky. This evaluation occurs before conscious reasoning begins and strongly influences what options are even considered.

Emotions play a central role in unconscious influence. Emotional experiences are stored not as verbal memories but as bodily and psychological states. When a current situation resembles a past experience, the associated emotional response is automatically activated. This can lead to attraction, avoidance, anxiety, or motivation without any conscious understanding of the cause. Over time, these emotional responses become reliable predictors of behavior, guiding action more consistently than conscious reasoning.

The unconscious also governs identity-based behavior. Individuals develop internalized beliefs about who they are and what they are capable of, often formed early in life. These beliefs operate quietly, shaping behavior to remain consistent with self-image. A person who unconsciously identifies as "not confident" may avoid opportunities despite consciously wanting success. The behavior feels natural, even inevitable, because it aligns with an internal narrative that is rarely questioned.

Conscious drivers, by contrast, tend to function after action rather than before it. The conscious mind frequently explains behavior retrospectively, constructing logical justifications for actions that were already initiated unconsciously. This creates the illusion that decisions were made consciously when, in fact, the conscious explanation is a narrative layered on top of an automatic process. This phenomenon helps preserve a sense of agency but obscures the true origins of behavior.

Despite their dominance, unconscious drivers are not immutable. Conscious awareness can influence behavior by interrupting automatic patterns and creating space for deliberate choice. However, this requires more than intention. It demands sustained attention, emotional regulation, and repetition. Conscious effort must be applied repeatedly until new patterns are encoded into the unconscious system. Only then does change feel natural rather than forced.

Understanding the distinction between conscious and unconscious drivers is essential for meaningful behavioral change. Without this understanding, individuals often blame themselves for lacking discipline or motivation, when the real issue lies in unseen psychological mechanisms. By recognizing that most actions originate beneath awareness, people can shift their focus from self-judgment to self-understanding.

Human action is not governed by a single decision-maker but by a layered system in which conscious and unconscious processes constantly interact. Conscious thought provides direction and meaning, while unconscious systems supply momentum and execution. When these systems are aligned, action feels effortless. When they are in conflict, behavior becomes inconsistent and frustrating. Mastery of action, therefore, begins not with control, but with awareness of the hidden drivers that shape behavior long before choice is felt.

Psychological Triggers Behind Behavior

Human behavior rarely arises in isolation. Every action is preceded by a stimulus—something that activates a response within the psychological system. These stimuli, known as psychological triggers, operate largely outside conscious awareness yet exert a powerful influence over behavior. A trigger can be an external event, an internal emotional state, a memory, a social cue, or even a thought. Once activated, it initiates a chain reaction that leads to action, often before conscious reasoning has time to intervene.

At the most basic level, psychological triggers function as signals. The mind constantly scans the environment and internal states for information relevant to safety, reward, and belonging. When a trigger is detected, the brain rapidly assesses its significance based on past experiences. This assessment happens automatically, drawing on emotional memory rather than rational analysis. If a trigger is associated with pleasure, comfort, or success, it encourages approach behavior. If it is associated with threat, failure, or pain, it prompts avoidance or defensive action.

Emotional triggers are among the most influential. Emotions are not simply reactions; they are adaptive signals designed to prepare the body for action. Fear triggers withdrawal or protection, anger triggers confrontation, and desire triggers pursuit. These responses occur quickly because they are rooted in survival mechanisms. Even in modern contexts where physical survival is not at risk, emotional triggers continue to guide behavior as if the stakes were immediate and significant. A critical comment, for example, can trigger a stress response that mirrors physical danger, leading to defensiveness or withdrawal.

Memory-based triggers also play a critical role. Experiences that carry emotional intensity are stored in memory networks that link situations, feelings, and outcomes. When a current situation resembles a past experience, the associated emotional and behavioral response is automatically reactivated. This process explains why certain environments, people, or even tones of voice can evoke strong reactions without a clear conscious explanation. The mind is not responding to the present moment alone but to a pattern it recognizes from the past.

Environmental triggers shape behavior through repetition and association. Specific locations, objects, or routines can become cues for automatic action. For instance, a familiar setting may trigger habitual behaviors without conscious planning. These triggers are reinforced through repeated exposure, gradually strengthening the connection between the cue and the response. Over time, the presence of the trigger alone is enough to initiate behavior, even when the original motivation is no longer relevant.

Social triggers are equally powerful. Human beings are deeply influenced by social context, approval, and perceived norms. Facial expressions, body language, authority signals, and group dynamics can all act as triggers that shape behavior. The desire for acceptance and fear of rejection are deeply embedded psychological drivers. As a result, individuals often adjust their behavior automatically in response to social cues, conforming to expectations even when they conflict with personal values or intentions.

Belief-based triggers operate at a more abstract level. Deeply held beliefs about oneself and the world function as internal triggers that influence interpretation and response. A belief such as "I am not good enough" can trigger hesitation, self-doubt, or avoidance in challenging situations. These triggers are particularly powerful because they shape perception before conscious evaluation occurs. The individual experiences the resulting behavior as logical or inevitable, unaware that it was activated by an unexamined belief.

Stress and fatigue amplify the influence of psychological triggers. When cognitive resources are depleted, the mind relies more heavily on automatic responses. In such states, triggers that might otherwise be managed consciously gain greater control over behavior. This explains why people often revert to familiar habits under pressure, even when those habits are counterproductive. The brain prioritizes efficiency over reflection when energy is low.

Importantly, psychological triggers are not inherently negative. They enable rapid responses, learning, and adaptation. Problems arise when triggers are outdated, misaligned with current goals, or rooted in unresolved emotional experiences. Because they operate automatically, these triggers can perpetuate behaviors that no longer serve the individual.

Awareness is the first step in changing the influence of psychological triggers. By identifying the cues that precede certain behaviors, individuals can begin to disrupt automatic patterns. This does not require eliminating triggers but understanding their function and modifying the response. When a trigger is recognized, conscious choice gains the opportunity to intervene.

Ultimately, psychological triggers reveal that behavior is not random or irrational. It is patterned, predictable, and meaningful within the context of the mind's learning history. By uncovering the triggers behind action, individuals gain insight into why they behave as they do and how those behaviors can be reshaped with intention.

How Decisions Form Beneath Awareness

Human decision-making is commonly experienced as a conscious act. A person considers options, evaluates consequences, and selects a course of action. While this experience feels deliberate, it represents only the visible endpoint of a much deeper psychological process. In reality, decisions begin forming long before conscious awareness registers that a choice is being made. Beneath the surface, the mind is continuously processing information, weighing emotional significance, and preparing responses automatically.

At the unconscious level, the brain operates as a predictive system. It constantly anticipates outcomes based on prior experiences, patterns, and learned associations. When a situation arises, the unconscious mind immediately compares it to similar past events and retrieves stored emotional and behavioral responses. This comparison happens rapidly and without language. By the time conscious thought engages, the mind has already generated a preferred direction of action.

Emotion is central to this hidden decision-making process. Emotional evaluations occur faster than rational analysis and provide the brain with quick judgments about what feels safe, rewarding, or threatening. These emotional signals bias attention and narrow the range of perceived options. A choice that feels emotionally uncomfortable may never be seriously considered, even if it is logically sound. Conversely, a choice associated with emotional relief or familiarity may feel "right" despite potential drawbacks.

Memory further shapes decisions beneath awareness. The mind does not store experiences as isolated facts but as interconnected networks linking context, emotion, and outcome. When a present situation activates a memory network, it brings with it the emotional tone and behavioral tendencies of the past experience. This activation influences judgment and preference without entering conscious awareness. The individual experiences the resulting inclination as intuition or instinct, unaware of its origin.

Cognitive shortcuts, known as heuristics, also guide unconscious decision formation. These mental rules simplify complex environments by relying on past patterns rather than exhaustive analysis. While heuristics improve efficiency, they can also introduce bias. Decisions influenced by familiarity, availability, or emotional intensity may feel justified, even when they are based on incomplete or distorted information. Because these shortcuts operate automatically, their influence often goes unnoticed.

Identity plays a subtle but powerful role in shaping decisions beneath awareness. Individuals tend to choose options that align with their self-concept and avoid those that threaten it. This alignment occurs automatically, filtering choices before conscious deliberation begins. A person who unconsciously identifies as cautious may reject opportunities that require risk, even when consciously desiring change. The decision feels consistent and reasonable, masking the identity-based influence at work.

Social conditioning further contributes to unconscious decision-making. Norms, expectations, and authority cues become internalized over time, guiding behavior even in the absence of external pressure. When faced with a decision, the mind automatically considers what is acceptable, expected, or rewarded within a social context. These considerations shape preference before conscious reasoning enters the process.

Importantly, conscious thought often functions as an interpreter rather than an initiator. After a decision tendency has already formed, the conscious mind constructs explanations that make the choice appear rational and intentional. This narrative preserves a sense of agency but obscures the underlying automatic processes. As a result, individuals may believe they made a decision logically when it was largely driven by unconscious factors.

Stress and cognitive load increase reliance on unconscious decision-making. When mental resources are limited, the brain prioritizes speed and familiarity. In such states, decisions are more strongly influenced by habit, emotion, and prior learning. This explains why individuals under pressure often revert to familiar choices, even when those choices conflict with long-term goals.

Understanding how decisions form beneath awareness shifts the focus from willpower to awareness. Behavioral change does not begin with forcing better choices but with recognizing the hidden processes that shape preference. By bringing these processes into conscious awareness, individuals can interrupt automatic patterns and create space for intentional decision-making.

Decisions are not sudden events but outcomes of ongoing psychological activity. What appears as a moment of choice is the final expression of processes that have been unfolding silently beneath awareness. Recognizing this reality is essential for understanding human behavior and for developing the capacity to act with greater clarity, consistency, and purpose.

Chapter 2

Motivation Beyond Desire

Motivation is commonly described as the force that moves people toward action. It is often reduced to desire—wanting something strongly enough to pursue it. While desire plays a role in initiating behavior, it rarely sustains it. Many people want success, change, or improvement, yet their actions remain inconsistent or short-lived. This gap between wanting and doing reveals a fundamental truth: motivation is more complex than desire alone.

This chapter explores motivation as a multi-layered psychological system shaped by internal drives, external pressures, meaning, and identity. Human beings are influenced not only by what they want, but by why they want it and what psychological forces are attached to that desire. Some motivations arise from within, driven by curiosity, mastery, and personal satisfaction. Others are imposed from outside, shaped by rewards, punishment, approval, or social expectation. These forces interact continuously, strengthening or weakening action depending on context.

At the center of sustained motivation lies meaning. When actions are connected to a deeper sense of purpose, they generate psychological energy that desire alone cannot provide. Meaning transforms effort into commitment and struggle into direction. Without meaning, motivation becomes fragile, easily disrupted by discomfort, boredom, or doubt. This explains why externally motivated goals often collapse once rewards are removed or obstacles appear.

The chapter also challenges the assumption that stronger desire guarantees action. Wanting can coexist with avoidance, hesitation, and self-sabotage when unconscious fears, conflicting values, or identity-based limitations are present. Motivation fails not because desire is weak, but because competing psychological forces outweigh it.

By examining intrinsic and extrinsic influences, the role of purpose, and the limits of desire, this chapter reframes motivation as a dynamic psychological process rather than a simple emotional state. Understanding this process is essential for translating intention into consistent, meaningful action.

Intrinsic and Extrinsic Forces

Motivation is often spoken of as a single internal drive, yet in practice it emerges from two distinct psychological forces: intrinsic and extrinsic motivation. These forces operate simultaneously, influencing not only whether a person takes action, but how long that action is sustained and how it is experienced. Understanding the difference between them is essential for explaining why some efforts feel energizing and self-sustaining, while others feel draining, fragile, and dependent on external reinforcement.

Intrinsic motivation arises from within the individual. It is driven by interest, curiosity, enjoyment, mastery, and personal satisfaction. When a person is intrinsically motivated, the activity itself provides psychological reward. The action feels meaningful, engaging, or aligned with personal values. This type of motivation does not require constant reminders or incentives because the experience of acting is reinforcing in its own right. People who pursue goals intrinsically often describe a sense of flow, absorption, or fulfillment that carries them forward even in the absence of immediate results.

At a psychological level, intrinsic motivation is closely linked to autonomy, competence, and identity. Autonomy refers to the sense of choice and self-direction. When individuals feel that they are acting by their own volition, motivation strengthens. Competence involves the perception of progress and skill development. As people experience improvement, motivation deepens. Identity plays a role by aligning action with self-concept; when behavior reflects who a person believes they are, persistence feels natural rather than forced.

Extrinsic motivation, in contrast, originates outside the individual. It is driven by rewards, punishments, recognition, deadlines, and social pressure. Money, grades, praise, approval, and fear of consequences are common extrinsic motivators. These forces are effective at initiating action, particularly in structured environments where compliance is required. However, extrinsic motivation often lacks durability. Once the external incentive is removed or loses its impact, behavior tends to diminish or stop altogether.

The psychological mechanism behind extrinsic motivation is contingency. Behavior is performed not for its own sake, but to achieve a separate outcome or avoid a negative one. This creates a transactional relationship with action. While this can be useful in certain contexts, it can also undermine long-term engagement. When individuals begin to associate effort solely with external outcomes, the internal value of the activity weakens. Over time, this can lead to dependency on incentives and reduced intrinsic interest.

The interaction between intrinsic and extrinsic forces is complex. In some cases, extrinsic motivators can support intrinsic motivation by providing structure, feedback, or initial engagement. In other cases, they can diminish it by shifting focus away from internal satisfaction toward external validation. When people feel controlled rather than supported, motivation becomes fragile and compliance-driven rather than self-directed.

One of the most significant limitations of extrinsic motivation is its vulnerability to resistance and burnout. Actions driven primarily by external pressure often generate stress and psychological fatigue. The individual may comply, but the effort feels heavy and unsustainable. This explains why many people achieve short-term results under pressure but struggle to maintain progress once external demands ease.

Intrinsic motivation, while more sustainable, is not immune to disruption. It can be weakened by environments that limit autonomy, devalue effort, or overemphasize outcomes. Additionally, not all necessary actions are inherently enjoyable. This creates a challenge: how to sustain motivation when intrinsic interest is low and extrinsic pressure is insufficient or undesirable.

The solution lies in integration rather than opposition. Effective motivation often emerges when extrinsic goals are internalized—when external demands are connected to personal meaning and identity. This internalization transforms obligation into choice. For example, a person may initially pursue a goal for external reasons, but over time adopt it as part of their self-concept. At that point, the motivation shifts from external enforcement to internal commitment.

Understanding intrinsic and extrinsic forces also reveals why desire alone is unreliable. Desire can be intense yet fleeting if it is not supported by intrinsic meaning or reinforced appropriately. Extrinsic rewards can spark desire but fail to sustain action without internal alignment. Lasting motivation depends on the balance between these forces and the extent to which they support rather than undermine one another.

Motivation, therefore, is not about choosing between intrinsic and extrinsic forces, but about recognizing their roles and limitations. Intrinsic motivation provides depth, resilience, and satisfaction. Extrinsic motivation provides structure, urgency, and direction. When aligned thoughtfully, they create a psychological environment in which action is not only possible, but sustainable.

The Role of Meaning and Purpose

Meaning and purpose occupy a central position in human motivation, extending far beyond simple desire or external reward. While people can act briefly out of obligation, fear, or impulse, sustained and resilient action almost always depends on a sense that what one is doing matters. Meaning provides psychological depth to behavior, while purpose offers direction. Together, they transform effort from something that must be forced into something that feels worth sustaining.

At a psychological level, meaning answers the question of *why* an action is undertaken. Purpose answers the question of *where* that action is leading. When these questions remain unresolved, motivation becomes unstable. Individuals may begin tasks with enthusiasm but quickly lose momentum when challenges arise. In contrast, when actions are grounded in meaning and connected to a clear purpose, persistence becomes more likely, even under difficulty.

Meaning is not inherent in activities themselves; it is constructed by the mind. Two people can perform the same action and experience it entirely differently based on the meaning they assign to it. One may perceive it as a burden, the other as an investment. This interpretation directly affects emotional engagement and willingness to continue. Meaning acts as a psychological lens, shaping how effort, discomfort, and delay are experienced.

Purpose adds a future-oriented dimension to motivation. It links present action to a larger narrative or outcome. When individuals can see how their current efforts contribute to a broader goal, short-term sacrifices become tolerable. Purpose organizes behavior over time, reducing impulsivity and providing a framework for decision-making. Without purpose, actions tend to fragment, driven by immediate pressures rather than long-term intention.

Research and observation consistently show that people with a strong sense of purpose demonstrate higher levels of resilience. They are better able to endure stress, recover from setbacks, and maintain focus. This is because purpose stabilizes motivation when emotional states fluctuate. On days when energy is low or confidence is shaken, purpose serves as an anchor, reminding the individual why continued effort matters.

Meaning also plays a crucial role in identity formation. When actions align with personal values and beliefs, they reinforce a coherent sense of self. This alignment strengthens motivation by making behavior feel authentic rather than imposed. Conversely, when actions conflict with internal values, resistance emerges, often unconsciously. The individual may procrastinate, disengage, or sabotage progress without fully understanding why.

Importantly, meaning does not require grand ideals. It can be found in personal growth, contribution, responsibility, or mastery. What matters is that the meaning resonates internally. External definitions of success or purpose often fail to motivate because they lack personal relevance. When purpose is borrowed rather than chosen, motivation becomes dependent on external validation and vulnerable to collapse.

The absence of meaning and purpose explains why desire alone is insufficient. Desire is reactive and emotionally driven. It fluctuates based on mood, circumstance, and stimulation. Meaning and purpose, by contrast, are cognitive structures that provide continuity. They allow individuals to act consistently even when desire fades. This distinction explains why disciplined action often persists in the absence of immediate gratification.

Modern environments frequently undermine meaning by emphasizing speed, comparison, and external metrics. When success is measured solely by outcomes rather than process or values, motivation becomes brittle. Individuals may achieve goals yet feel disengaged or empty, leading to cycles of achievement without fulfillment. Reconnecting action to meaning restores psychological depth and intrinsic engagement.

Cultivating meaning and purpose requires reflection rather than intensity. It involves examining values, clarifying priorities, and consciously linking actions to broader intentions. This process does not eliminate difficulty but reframes it. Effort becomes part of a chosen path rather than an imposed burden.

In the architecture of motivation, meaning and purpose function as stabilizing forces. They do not replace desire or external incentives, but they contextualize them. When meaning is present, action gains resilience. When purpose is clear, effort gains direction. Together, they provide the psychological foundation for motivation that endures beyond momentary impulse or reward.

Why Wanting Is Not Enough

Desire is often treated as the starting point of action. People assume that if they want something badly enough, behavior will naturally follow. This assumption is deeply ingrained in cultural narratives that equate success with passion and failure with insufficient desire. Yet in practice, wanting is one of the least reliable predictors of sustained action. Many individuals want change intensely, yet remain trapped in the same patterns. This disconnect reveals a critical psychological reality: wanting initiates intention, but it does not guarantee execution.

One reason wanting fails is that desire is emotionally driven and inherently unstable. It fluctuates with mood, energy, and circumstance. What feels compelling in one moment can lose urgency in another. When action depends solely on emotional intensity, consistency becomes impossible. The mind naturally avoids discomfort and seeks immediate relief, even when long-term goals are valued. As a result, desire is easily overridden by competing emotional forces such as fear, anxiety, or the need for comfort.

Another limitation of wanting is its inability to overcome unconscious resistance. Beneath conscious desire often lie hidden fears, conflicting beliefs, or identity-based constraints. A person may want success yet fear exposure, responsibility, or failure. These unconscious concerns generate avoidance behaviors that quietly counteract desire. Because the resistance is not fully conscious, the individual experiences confusion and self-blame rather than clarity.

Wanting also fails when it is not supported by structure. Desire provides direction but not organization. Without clear systems, habits, and environmental support, motivation dissipates under friction. The mind defaults to familiar routines, especially under stress or fatigue. In such conditions, desire alone cannot compete with deeply ingrained behavioral patterns that require less cognitive effort.

Additionally, wanting often focuses on outcomes rather than processes. People want results—achievement, recognition, change—but may not fully engage with the actions required to reach them. When progress is slow or invisible, motivation collapses. This outcome fixation disconnects effort from reward, making persistence psychologically difficult. Sustainable action requires engagement with the process itself, not just the imagined endpoint.

Social and environmental factors further limit the power of wanting. Individuals operate within contexts shaped by norms, expectations, and constraints. A strong personal desire may still be undermined by environments that discourage change or reinforce old behaviors. Without adjusting these contexts, desire must constantly fight against external pressure, a battle it rarely wins.

Importantly, wanting does not automatically translate into readiness. Change requires not only desire but psychological capacity. Stress, cognitive overload, and emotional depletion reduce the ability to act, regardless of how strongly one wants an outcome. In such states, the brain prioritizes energy conservation and immediate relief over long-term goals. Wanting remains present, but action becomes inaccessible.

This misunderstanding often leads to moralizing motivation. When people fail to act, they are told to want it more, try harder, or increase discipline. This approach overlooks the underlying psychological mechanisms that govern behavior. It treats motivation as a character trait rather than a system influenced by emotion, identity, habit, and environment.

Sustainable action emerges when wanting is integrated with meaning, structure, and awareness. Desire must be anchored in purpose, supported by habits, and aligned with identity. When these elements are present, action no longer depends on emotional intensity alone. It becomes resilient to fluctuation and capable of enduring discomfort.

Recognizing that wanting is not enough is not discouraging; it is liberating. It shifts the focus from self-judgment to system design. Instead of asking, "Why don't I want this badly enough?" individuals can ask, "What is interfering with my ability to act?" This question opens the door to practical change.

Ultimately, wanting is a signal, not a solution. It indicates direction but does not supply the mechanisms required for movement. Understanding this distinction allows individuals to build motivation that is grounded, structured, and sustainable—transforming intention into consistent action rather than fleeting desire.

Chapter 3

The Power of Habitual Thinking

Human beings often assume that their thoughts are spontaneous and deliberate, yet much of thinking itself is habitual. Just as the body learns repeated movements, the mind learns repeated ways of interpreting, responding to, and anticipating the world. These mental patterns develop gradually through experience, reinforcement, and repetition, eventually operating with little conscious effort. Once established, they shape perception, emotion, and action in ways that feel automatic and natural.

Habitual thinking exists because the brain is designed for efficiency. Continuously evaluating every situation from scratch would be cognitively exhausting. Instead, the mind forms shortcuts—predictable thought patterns that allow rapid response to familiar situations. These patterns are not inherently harmful; they enable learning, skill development, and adaptation. However, when they go unexamined, they can quietly limit growth and lock individuals into repetitive behavioral loops.

This chapter examines how mental habits form and why they exert such a powerful influence over behavior. Thought patterns often originate in emotionally charged experiences, early learning, or repeated environmental cues. Over time, they become default interpretations that shape how situations are perceived before conscious reasoning begins. A challenge may automatically be seen as a threat, criticism as rejection, or uncertainty as failure—each triggering predictable emotional and behavioral responses.

Habitual thinking also explains why change feels difficult even when motivation is high. New intentions must compete with deeply ingrained mental routines that require less effort and feel familiar. Under stress or fatigue, the mind almost always returns to these defaults, reinforcing the cycle.

By understanding the structure of habitual thinking, individuals gain insight into how automatic responses are learned and maintained. This awareness creates the possibility of interruption—of breaking old loops and intentionally rebuilding new ones. The chapter sets the foundation for recognizing that lasting change begins not with force, but with reshaping the patterns that quietly govern thought and action.

How Mental Patterns Are Formed

Mental patterns are the invisible frameworks through which the mind interprets experience and guides behavior. They are not created deliberately; rather, they emerge gradually as the brain learns to respond efficiently to recurring situations. Every repeated thought, emotional reaction, or behavioral response strengthens certain neural pathways, making those responses more likely to occur again. Over time, these pathways become default routes the mind follows automatically, shaping perception and action without conscious instruction.

At the foundation of mental pattern formation is repetition. When the mind encounters similar situations repeatedly, it begins to anticipate outcomes based on prior experience. This anticipation reduces cognitive effort by allowing quick interpretation rather than careful analysis. The brain prioritizes speed and efficiency, especially in familiar contexts. As a result, initial reactions often bypass conscious reasoning and rely instead on learned patterns that have proven useful in the past.

Emotion plays a critical role in this process. Experiences associated with strong emotions—whether positive or negative—are encoded more deeply than neutral ones. Fear, pleasure, shame, excitement, and relief all act as intensifiers, strengthening the mental associations connected to an event. When similar situations arise later, the emotional memory is automatically reactivated, guiding thought and behavior in predictable ways. This mechanism helps explain why certain responses feel instinctive rather than chosen.

Early experiences are particularly influential in shaping mental patterns. During formative periods, the brain is highly adaptive, absorbing information about safety, relationships, and self-worth. Interpretations formed during these stages often persist into adulthood, even when circumstances change. A child who learns to associate mistakes with rejection may develop a habitual pattern of self-criticism or avoidance.

Although the original context may no longer exist, the pattern remains active, guiding adult behavior.

Social learning further reinforces mental habits. Humans learn not only from direct experience but also through observation and feedback. Reactions from caregivers, peers, and authority figures signal which behaviors are rewarded or discouraged. Over time, these signals become internalized, shaping internal dialogue and expectations. The mind adopts patterns that increase acceptance and reduce conflict, often without conscious awareness of why certain reactions feel natural.

Language also contributes to pattern formation. The words individuals use to describe themselves and their experiences shape internal narratives. Repeated self-statements—such as "I always fail" or "I am not good at this"—become cognitive templates that influence perception. These linguistic patterns guide attention, emphasizing evidence that confirms the narrative while filtering out contradictory information. In this way, mental patterns become self-reinforcing.

Cognitive shortcuts, or heuristics, accelerate pattern formation by simplifying complex environments. Rather than evaluating every new situation objectively, the mind categorizes experiences based on similarity. While this saves energy, it also reduces flexibility. Once a category is formed, new information is interpreted through that lens, even when it no longer accurately reflects reality. This rigidity explains why outdated mental patterns persist despite conscious efforts to change them.

Stress and repetition further solidify mental habits. Under pressure, the brain defaults to familiar responses that require less cognitive effort. Each repetition strengthens the existing pattern, making it more accessible in the future. Over time, this creates a cycle in which stress reinforces habitual thinking, and habitual thinking increases vulnerability to stress.

Importantly, mental patterns are adaptive by design. They allow individuals to navigate the world efficiently and respond quickly to recurring challenges. Problems arise when these patterns are misaligned with current goals or environments. A response that once provided protection or efficiency may later restrict growth or well-being.

Awareness is the first step in reshaping mental patterns. By recognizing that thoughts are learned responses rather than objective truths, individuals create distance between experience and interpretation. This awareness interrupts automaticity, making alternative responses possible.

Mental patterns are not fixed traits; they are learned systems. With deliberate attention, emotional regulation, and repeated practice, new patterns can be formed. Change does not occur by suppressing old habits, but by consistently reinforcing new ways of thinking that better serve present goals. Understanding how mental patterns form reveals that transformation is not a matter of force, but of learning—learning to guide the mind rather than be guided by it.

Automatic Responses and Learned Behavior

Much of human behavior unfolds automatically, without deliberate thought or conscious intention. These automatic responses are not random; they are learned behaviors shaped through repeated interaction with the environment. Over time, the mind identifies patterns in experience and builds responses that can be activated quickly and efficiently. This process allows individuals to function in complex environments without constant cognitive effort, but it also explains why behavior often feels habitual and resistant to change.

Automatic responses develop through learning mechanisms that associate specific cues with particular outcomes. When an action leads to relief, reward, or avoidance of discomfort, the mind records this connection. The next time a similar cue appears, the response is activated automatically. This learning does not require conscious awareness; it occurs through repetition and reinforcement. As a result, behavior becomes increasingly efficient but less flexible.

Conditioning plays a central role in shaping learned behavior. Through classical conditioning, neutral stimuli become linked to emotional responses. A tone of voice, facial expression, or environment can trigger emotional reactions based on past associations. Through operant conditioning, behaviors are strengthened or weakened depending on their consequences. Actions that are rewarded are repeated, while those that lead to discomfort are avoided. Over time, these conditioned responses become embedded in the behavioral repertoire.

Emotional learning further accelerates automaticity. Emotions act as powerful reinforcers, encoding experiences in ways that prioritize survival and efficiency. When an emotional response is paired repeatedly with a particular situation, the emotional reaction becomes a cue for action. This explains why people often respond emotionally before they can articulate a reason. The behavior feels immediate and justified, even when it conflicts with conscious intention.

Automatic responses are also shaped by cognitive habits. Repeated patterns of thought—such as interpreting uncertainty as threat or criticism as rejection—become default interpretations. These interpretations trigger predictable emotional and behavioral responses. Over time, the sequence becomes seamless: a situation arises, a thought pattern activates, an emotion follows, and action occurs. The entire process can unfold without conscious reflection.

Social learning contributes significantly to learned behavior. From early childhood, individuals observe others and internalize behavioral norms. Reactions modeled by caregivers, peers, and authority figures become templates for response. Approval and disapproval guide learning, reinforcing behaviors that align with social expectations. Eventually, these external influences are internalized, guiding behavior even in the absence of observation.

Habit formation represents a specific form of learned automatic behavior. Habits emerge when actions are repeated in stable contexts. The brain associates a cue with a routine and an outcome, forming a loop that requires minimal conscious input. Once established, habits are triggered by the cue itself, regardless of the original motivation. This efficiency is advantageous, but it also explains why habits persist even when they are no longer desirable.

Stress and cognitive load increase reliance on automatic responses. When mental resources are depleted, the brain prioritizes speed and familiarity. Deliberate control weakens, and learned behaviors dominate. This is why individuals under pressure often revert to old habits, even after periods of successful change. Automatic responses require less energy, making them the default under strain.

Importantly, automatic responses are not inherently negative. They allow skill acquisition, efficiency, and rapid adaptation. Problems arise when learned behaviors are outdated or misaligned with current goals. Because they operate below awareness, these responses can produce outcomes that feel uncontrollable or self-sabotaging.

Change begins with recognition. Identifying the cues that trigger automatic behavior reveals the structure of learned responses. Rather than attempting to eliminate habits, effective change involves redesigning the response to familiar cues. By introducing conscious awareness at the point of activation, individuals create an opportunity to choose differently.

Automatic responses and learned behavior demonstrate that action is not a simple product of willpower. It is the outcome of learning histories, emotional reinforcement, and environmental structure. Understanding this process shifts the focus from self-blame to self-observation. When behavior is seen as learned rather than inherent, it becomes something that can be modified, redirected, and rebuilt with intention.

Breaking and Rebuilding Action Loops

Action loops are recurring sequences of cue, response, and outcome that govern much of human behavior. Once established, these loops operate automatically, guiding action with minimal conscious effort. They are efficient, predictable, and deeply ingrained. However, when an action loop produces outcomes that no longer serve the individual, it can become a source of frustration and stagnation. Breaking and rebuilding these loops is essential for meaningful behavioral change, yet it is often misunderstood as a matter of willpower rather than psychological design.

To understand how action loops can be changed, it is first necessary to recognize why they persist. The brain favors familiar patterns because they conserve energy and reduce uncertainty. Each repetition strengthens the neural pathways associated with the loop, making activation faster and more likely. Even negative outcomes can reinforce a loop if they provide predictability or emotional relief. This explains why people often repeat behaviors they consciously wish to avoid.

Breaking an action loop does not begin with stopping the behavior. Attempts to suppress a habit without understanding its function usually fail. The loop exists because it fulfills a psychological need, such as comfort, control, distraction, or emotional regulation. Until this need is identified, the mind will resist change and default to the familiar pattern.

The first step in breaking an action loop is awareness. This involves identifying the cue that initiates the loop and the outcome that reinforces it. Cues can be internal, such as emotional states or thoughts, or external, such as environments, time of day, or social interactions. Outcomes are not always tangible rewards; they may include relief from discomfort, reduction of anxiety, or a sense of familiarity. Recognizing these elements transforms the loop from an unconscious process into an observable system.

Once awareness is established, interruption becomes possible. Interruption does not require eliminating the cue; it requires altering the response. When a cue is encountered, creating a pause allows conscious choice to enter the process. This pause weakens automaticity by disrupting the seamless progression from trigger to action. Even small interruptions, repeated consistently, can reduce the strength of an old loop over time.

Rebuilding an action loop involves designing a new response that satisfies the same underlying need but produces a more constructive outcome. This is a critical principle: the brain resists loops that leave needs unmet. A replacement behavior must be realistic, accessible, and emotionally satisfying. If the new response requires excessive effort or fails to deliver psychological reward, the old loop will regain dominance.

Repetition is essential in rebuilding loops. New responses must be practiced consistently in the presence of the original cue. Each repetition strengthens new neural pathways, gradually increasing their accessibility. During this phase, lapses are common and should not be interpreted as failure. They are part of the learning process. The brain is adapting, not obeying commands.

Environment plays a powerful role in loop reconstruction. Small changes in context can reduce exposure to triggers or support new responses. Adjusting surroundings, routines, or social influences lowers the cognitive load required to sustain change. Rather than relying on constant self-control, effective loop rebuilding designs conditions that make desired behavior easier and undesired behavior harder.

Emotional regulation also supports loop change. Many action loops are driven by unmanaged emotional states. Developing the ability to tolerate discomfort without immediate relief reduces dependence on old patterns. This skill strengthens the capacity to remain present during the pause between cue and response, increasing behavioral flexibility.

Importantly, identity influences loop durability. When new behaviors are integrated into self-concept, they become self-reinforcing. A person who begins to see themselves as someone who responds differently strengthens commitment to the new loop. Identity-based reinforcement provides stability when motivation fluctuates.

Breaking and rebuilding action loops is not about erasing the past. Old patterns rarely disappear entirely; they become less dominant. The goal is not perfection but flexibility—the ability to respond intentionally rather than automatically. Through awareness, interruption, and consistent reinforcement, action loops can be reshaped.

Ultimately, behavior changes when systems change. Action loops reveal that human behavior is structured, learnable, and adaptable. By working with this structure rather than against it, individuals can redesign their patterns of action in ways that align with purpose, values, and long-term well-being.

Chapter 4

Emotion as a Catalyst for Action

Emotion is often treated as a disruption to rational thinking, something to be controlled or minimized in the pursuit of good decisions. In reality, emotion is not an obstacle to action—it is one of its primary drivers. Long before conscious reasoning evaluates options, emotional processes assign value, urgency, and meaning to experience. These emotional evaluations shape attention, narrow or expand perceived choices, and determine whether action feels compelling or avoidable.

This chapter explores emotion as a source of psychological energy that propels behavior. Emotions signal what matters, highlighting potential threats and rewards in the environment. Fear can mobilize protective action or induce paralysis. Pleasure reinforces repetition and guides pursuit. Even subtle emotional states influence decision-making by biasing judgment and preference. Action, therefore, is rarely neutral; it is charged with emotional significance that influences both speed and direction.

Emotion also plays a central role in avoidance. Many behaviors are shaped less by the pursuit of pleasure than by the desire to reduce discomfort. Avoidance behaviors often operate quietly, disguised as procrastination, distraction, or rational delay. These patterns persist because they provide short-term emotional relief, even when they undermine long-term goals. Understanding avoidance requires examining the emotional costs and rewards that accompany behavior.

The chapter further examines how emotional memory reinforces behavioral repetition. Experiences marked by strong emotion are encoded deeply and reactivated automatically in similar contexts. This reactivation influences behavior without conscious recall, creating cycles that feel instinctive rather than chosen. Emotional memory explains why certain patterns endure despite awareness and intention.

By reframing emotion as a catalyst rather than a complication, this chapter reveals its central role in human action. Recognizing how emotional energy, fear, pleasure, and memory shape behavior provides essential insight into why people act as they do—and how those actions can be redirected with awareness rather than resistance.

Emotional Energy and Decision-Making

Decision-making is often described as a rational process guided by logic, analysis, and conscious evaluation. While reasoning plays a role, it is rarely the engine that drives action. Beneath conscious thought lies emotional energy—the psychological force that gives decisions urgency, weight, and momentum. Without emotion, choices remain abstract and inert. Emotion transforms thought into movement, determining not only what people decide, but how quickly and decisively they act.

Emotional energy functions as a signal of importance. When a situation triggers emotion, it tells the mind that something meaningful is at stake. This signal directs attention, prioritizing certain information while filtering out the rest. Decisions that carry emotional weight rise to the foreground of awareness, while emotionally neutral options are often ignored. In this way, emotion shapes the decision landscape before conscious reasoning begins.

Different emotions generate different types of energy. Excitement and enthusiasm expand perception, increasing openness to possibility and risk. Anxiety narrows focus, emphasizing potential threats and uncertainties. Anger mobilizes action by increasing confidence and reducing hesitation. Each emotional state biases decision-making in predictable ways. These biases are not errors; they are adaptive responses designed to prepare the individual for action under specific conditions.

Importantly, emotional energy influences the speed of decisions. High emotional arousal accelerates choice, reducing deliberation in favor of immediate action. Low emotional engagement slows decision-making, often resulting in indecision or delay. This explains why people can act swiftly in emotionally charged situations yet struggle to decide when stakes feel unclear or disconnected from feeling.

Emotions also assign value to outcomes. Rational analysis may identify what is optimal, but emotion determines what feels worthwhile. A choice that aligns with emotional values feels compelling, even if it requires effort or sacrifice. Conversely, a choice that lacks emotional resonance may be postponed indefinitely, regardless of its logical merits. Emotional valuation is therefore central to motivation and follow-through.

The relationship between emotion and decision-making becomes especially evident in situations of conflict. When emotions compete—such as desire versus fear—the decision reflects the dominant emotional energy rather than conscious intention. A person may understand the benefits of action but still avoid it if fear carries greater emotional weight. This dynamic explains why knowledge alone does not produce change.

Emotional regulation plays a critical role in decision quality. When emotional energy becomes overwhelming, it can distort perception and impair judgment. High stress or intense fear can trigger impulsive decisions focused on immediate relief rather than long-term benefit. Conversely, suppressed or unacknowledged emotions can lead to indecision and disengagement. Effective decision-making does not require eliminating emotion but managing its intensity and influence.

Past emotional experiences shape current decisions through memory. The emotional outcomes of previous choices are stored and retrieved automatically, influencing future preferences. A decision that once led to emotional pain may be avoided, even when circumstances have changed. This learned emotional response operates beneath awareness, guiding behavior through anticipation rather than analysis.

Social emotions further complicate decision-making. Emotions such as shame, pride, and belonging influence choices in social contexts. Decisions are often shaped by anticipated emotional responses from others, such as approval or rejection. These social emotions can motivate conformity or resistance, depending on how identity and values are structured.

Crucially, emotional energy does not oppose rational thought; it enables it. Reason provides structure and clarity, but emotion supplies motivation and commitment. Decisions that integrate both are more likely to be executed consistently. When emotion and reason are misaligned, action becomes unstable, oscillating between impulse and hesitation.

Understanding emotional energy reframes decision-making as a dynamic psychological process rather than a purely logical one. It highlights why some choices feel effortless while others require constant effort. By recognizing how emotional energy shapes attention, value, and urgency, individuals gain insight into their own decision patterns.

Ultimately, decisions follow emotion. To change behavior, one must address the emotional forces that energize or inhibit action. When emotional energy is understood and directed rather than ignored, decision-making becomes more intentional, resilient, and aligned with purpose.

Fear, Pleasure, and Avoidance Behavior

Human behavior is profoundly shaped by two fundamental emotional forces: fear and pleasure. These forces do not merely influence action; they organize it. Much of what people do—or fail to do—can be traced to the pursuit of pleasure or the avoidance of fear. These emotional drivers operate quickly, often outside conscious awareness, creating behavioral patterns that feel automatic rather than chosen.

Fear is a protective mechanism designed to signal threat and mobilize survival responses. In its original biological context, fear prompted immediate action in the presence of danger. In modern life, however, fear is frequently triggered by psychological rather than physical threats. Fear of failure, rejection, loss of control, or uncertainty can activate the same stress responses as physical danger. When fear is triggered, attention narrows, risk tolerance decreases, and behavior becomes focused on safety rather than growth.

Avoidance behavior is one of the most common responses to fear. Instead of confronting a perceived threat, the individual disengages, delays, or distracts. Avoidance can take subtle forms, such as procrastination, overthinking, or rational delay. These behaviors provide short-term emotional relief by reducing anxiety, reinforcing the pattern. Each time avoidance successfully lowers discomfort, the mind learns that avoidance is effective, strengthening the behavior loop.

Pleasure functions as the counterpart to fear. It signals reward, satisfaction, and safety. Behaviors associated with pleasure are repeated because they generate positive emotional feedback. Pleasure reinforces habits, making certain actions feel desirable and self-sustaining. Even small pleasures, such as relief from stress or a sense of familiarity, can strongly reinforce behavior.

Importantly, pleasure is not limited to positive outcomes; it also includes relief from negative states. Many avoidance behaviors are reinforced not by joy, but by the pleasure of escaping discomfort. For example, avoiding a difficult task may produce temporary relief from anxiety, which the brain registers as a reward. This relief-based pleasure strengthens avoidance, even though it undermines long-term goals.

Fear and pleasure often interact, creating complex motivational dynamics. A behavior may promise pleasure but also trigger fear, leading to internal conflict. In such cases, the dominant emotion determines action. If fear outweighs anticipated pleasure, avoidance occurs. If pleasure outweighs fear, action proceeds. This balance is rarely conscious; it is determined by emotional intensity and learned associations.

Over time, repeated fear-based avoidance can narrow behavioral range. The individual begins to anticipate fear before it occurs, avoiding situations preemptively. This anticipation reinforces limiting beliefs and reduces exposure to corrective experiences that could weaken fear responses. The result is a self-perpetuating cycle in which avoidance maintains the very fears it seeks to escape.

Social and cultural influences shape fear and pleasure responses as well. Social rejection, embarrassment, or loss of status can trigger strong fear responses, leading to conformity or withdrawal. Conversely, social approval and belonging generate pleasure that reinforces compliance with group norms. These dynamics explain why individuals often prioritize social safety over personal growth.

Understanding avoidance behavior requires recognizing its function rather than judging it. Avoidance is not laziness or weakness; it is a learned strategy for emotional regulation. It persists because it works—at least in the short term. Long-term change requires developing alternative ways to manage fear and access reward.

Reducing avoidance involves increasing tolerance for discomfort and reshaping emotional associations. When individuals face feared situations gradually and experience manageable outcomes, fear responses weaken. Simultaneously, creating meaningful rewards for constructive behavior strengthens approach motivation. Over time, the emotional balance shifts, making action more likely.

Fear and pleasure are powerful forces, but they are not fixed. They are shaped by experience, interpretation, and learning. By understanding how these emotions drive avoidance behavior, individuals gain the ability to intervene consciously. Action becomes less about forcing courage and more about redesigning emotional responses.

Ultimately, behavior follows emotion. Avoidance persists when fear dominates and relief is rewarding. Change occurs when emotional systems are recalibrated to support engagement rather than escape. Recognizing this process transforms fear and pleasure from obstacles into tools for intentional action.

Emotional Memory and Behavioral Repetition

Human behavior is deeply influenced by emotional memory—the system through which emotionally charged experiences are stored, recalled, and reused by the mind. Unlike factual memory, emotional memory does not rely on conscious recall or narrative detail. It operates beneath awareness, shaping reactions, preferences, and actions automatically. This system exists to promote survival and efficiency, but it also explains why behaviors repeat even when individuals consciously want change.

When an experience is accompanied by strong emotion, the brain assigns it heightened significance. Emotional arousal strengthens memory encoding, linking the situation, emotional state, and behavioral response into a unified pattern. Later, when a similar situation arises, the emotional memory is reactivated automatically, producing a familiar feeling and prompting a familiar action. This process occurs rapidly and without conscious deliberation, creating the impression of instinct or intuition.

Behavioral repetition often begins with this automatic emotional activation. A person may feel anxious, defensive, or motivated without understanding why. The emotional state narrows attention and biases judgment, guiding behavior toward what previously reduced discomfort or increased reward. Over time, this repetition strengthens the emotional-behavioral link, making the response more likely to occur again.

Importantly, emotional memory does not evaluate whether a response is currently appropriate. It relies on past outcomes rather than present conditions. A response that once provided protection or relief may persist long after the original threat has disappeared. This explains why individuals may react strongly to situations that are objectively safe or benign. The emotional system is responding to a remembered pattern, not the current reality.

Avoidance behaviors are particularly reinforced by emotional memory. When a behavior successfully reduces emotional distress, the relief becomes part of the memory. The brain learns that avoidance works, reinforcing the pattern. Each repetition strengthens the association, making avoidance the default response. This process can occur without conscious intention, leading to persistent behavioral loops that resist change.

Emotional memory also reinforces positive behaviors. Actions associated with pride, belonging, or satisfaction are more likely to be repeated. These emotions serve as internal rewards, strengthening approach behavior. However, negative emotional memories often exert stronger influence because the brain prioritizes threat avoidance over reward pursuit. This asymmetry explains why fear-based patterns can be particularly resistant to change.

Social experiences play a significant role in emotional memory formation. Interactions involving acceptance, rejection, praise, or criticism are emotionally charged and deeply encoded. These memories shape future behavior in social contexts, influencing communication, risk-taking, and self-expression. A single intense social experience can establish patterns that persist for years.

Emotional memory is also linked to identity. Repeated emotional experiences contribute to beliefs about the self and the world. These beliefs, in turn, influence behavior by shaping expectation and interpretation. When emotional memory and identity align, behavioral repetition feels natural and justified, even when it is limiting.

Changing behavior requires engaging with emotional memory rather than ignoring it. Logical insight alone rarely alters emotional responses. New experiences must be paired with different emotional outcomes to weaken old associations. This process requires repetition and emotional regulation, allowing the mind to learn that alternative responses are safe and rewarding.

Awareness creates the initial space for change. Recognizing emotional triggers and their associated memories reduces automaticity. Gradual exposure to feared situations, paired with manageable emotional experiences, can update emotional memory. Over time, new associations form, and behavioral patterns shift.

Emotional memory explains why behavior is not simply a matter of choice. Actions repeat because the mind is applying what it has learned emotionally. By understanding this mechanism, individuals can approach change with patience rather than self-blame. Behavioral repetition becomes a signal of unresolved emotional learning, not personal failure.

Ultimately, emotional memory is a powerful teacher. It shapes behavior through experience rather than instruction. When guided intentionally, it can be retrained to support growth, resilience, and adaptive action.

Chapter 5

Belief Systems and Behavioral Control

Beliefs are often mistaken for opinions—flexible ideas that can be adjusted through reasoning or new information. In reality, beliefs function as psychological control systems that quietly govern perception, emotion, and action. They shape how individuals interpret experience, what they expect from the world, and what they believe is possible for themselves. Long before a decision feels conscious, belief systems are already guiding behavior by defining the boundaries of thought and action.

This chapter explores how beliefs form the internal framework through which behavior is regulated. Core beliefs—deeply held assumptions about the self, others, and life—emerge through early experiences, emotional learning, and repeated reinforcement. Once established, these beliefs become intertwined with identity, influencing behavior in ways that feel natural rather than chosen. People tend to act in alignment with who they believe they are, even when those beliefs limit growth or opportunity.

Belief systems also explain why knowledge alone rarely changes behavior. A person may understand what needs to be done yet feel unable to act because unconscious beliefs contradict conscious intention. These limiting beliefs operate as internal constraints, shaping motivation, confidence, and persistence. Because they function beneath awareness, their influence is often mistaken for reality rather than interpretation.

The chapter further examines how internal narratives—repeated stories individuals tell themselves—reinforce belief systems and sustain behavioral patterns. These narratives organize experience, justify action, and maintain consistency within identity. When left unexamined, they quietly reinforce the same outcomes.

By understanding how beliefs control behavior, individuals gain the ability to interrupt automatic patterns and reshape internal narratives. Change becomes possible not by forcing new actions, but by addressing the belief structures that determine what actions feel attainable. This chapter lays the foundation for understanding belief as a powerful driver of behavior—and a critical leverage point for intentional change.

Core Beliefs and Identity Formation

Core beliefs are the deepest assumptions individuals hold about themselves, others, and the nature of the world. They are not surface-level opinions or consciously chosen ideas; they are internalized conclusions formed through experience, emotion, and repetition. Once established, core beliefs function as psychological filters, shaping perception, guiding interpretation, and influencing behavior automatically. Over time, these beliefs become woven into identity, determining how individuals see themselves and how they believe they must act.

The formation of core beliefs begins early in life, when the brain is highly adaptive and sensitive to feedback. Experiences involving safety, attachment, success, failure, acceptance, or rejection carry strong emotional weight. The mind extracts meaning from these experiences, forming generalized conclusions such as "I am capable," "I am not enough," "People cannot be trusted," or "Effort leads to reward." These conclusions are rarely articulated at the time; they are absorbed implicitly through emotional learning.

Emotion plays a critical role in belief formation. Experiences paired with strong emotional responses are encoded more deeply than neutral events. When a particular interpretation repeatedly coincides with emotional relief or distress, it becomes reinforced as truth. Over time, the belief no longer feels like an interpretation—it feels like an objective fact about reality. This emotional reinforcement explains why core beliefs are resistant to change, even in the face of contradictory evidence.

As core beliefs solidify, they begin to shape identity. Identity is not a fixed trait but a narrative constructed from repeated beliefs about who one is. Individuals act in ways that confirm their self-concept, seeking consistency between belief and behavior. This consistency provides psychological stability, even when the belief is limiting. For example, a person who believes they are "not confident" may avoid situations that challenge this belief, reinforcing both the identity and the behavior.

Core beliefs also influence attention and memory. The mind naturally seeks information that confirms existing beliefs and filters out information that contradicts them. This confirmation bias strengthens identity by creating a self-reinforcing loop: beliefs guide perception, perception reinforces beliefs, and behavior aligns with both. Over time, alternative interpretations become less accessible, making change feel unrealistic or threatening.

Social environments further reinforce core beliefs and identity. Feedback from caregivers, peers, and authority figures often mirrors or amplifies internal beliefs. When social responses align with internal narratives, beliefs gain additional credibility. Conversely, when social feedback contradicts core beliefs, it is often dismissed or reinterpreted to preserve internal consistency. This dynamic illustrates how identity resists disruption.

Importantly, core beliefs influence motivation and action by defining perceived limits. They determine what goals feel attainable, what risks feel tolerable, and what efforts feel worthwhile. A belief such as "I fail when I try" undermines persistence by making effort feel futile. Conversely, a belief such as "I can learn through effort" supports resilience and growth. These beliefs operate automatically, shaping behavior before conscious intention is engaged.

Understanding core beliefs shifts the focus of change from behavior to interpretation. Attempts to modify behavior without addressing underlying beliefs often fail because the behavior conflicts with identity. The mind resists actions that threaten coherence, even when change is desired. Sustainable change requires updating the belief structures that support identity.

Reforming core beliefs does not involve denying past experience. It involves recognizing that beliefs are conclusions drawn from limited data rather than absolute truths. Through awareness, emotional processing, and new experiences, beliefs can be revised. As beliefs change, identity becomes more flexible, allowing new behaviors to feel authentic rather than forced.

Core beliefs and identity are powerful because they provide continuity and meaning. When examined consciously, they become tools rather than constraints. By understanding how beliefs form and shape identity, individuals gain the ability to redefine who they are and, in doing so, reshape how they act.

Limiting Beliefs That Shape Action

Limiting beliefs are deeply held assumptions that restrict perception, narrow possibility, and constrain behavior. They are not deliberate choices or conscious refusals to act; they are internalized conclusions about what is possible, safe, or appropriate. Because they operate beneath awareness, limiting beliefs often feel like objective truths rather than interpretations. As a result, they quietly shape action by defining invisible boundaries that behavior rarely crosses.

These beliefs typically form through repeated experiences, particularly those involving failure, rejection, or emotional distress. When an individual encounters a negative outcome and lacks the psychological tools to process it fully, the mind seeks meaning in order to predict and prevent future pain. The conclusion drawn becomes a belief, such as "I am not capable," "Effort leads to disappointment," or "Taking risks is dangerous." Once established, this belief functions as a protective mechanism, discouraging behaviors that might recreate the original discomfort.

Limiting beliefs influence action primarily by shaping expectation. Expectation determines effort. When the mind anticipates failure, embarrassment, or loss, motivation weakens and hesitation increases. Actions that challenge the belief feel emotionally costly, triggering anxiety or self-doubt. To avoid this discomfort, the individual unconsciously chooses behaviors that maintain emotional safety, even when those behaviors undermine long-term goals.

One of the most powerful ways limiting beliefs shape action is through avoidance. Avoidance does not always appear as inaction; it can take the form of procrastination, distraction, over-preparation, or rational delay. These behaviors provide plausible explanations that mask the underlying belief. The individual may appear busy or thoughtful while unconsciously protecting themselves from perceived threat. Each instance of avoidance reinforces the belief, strengthening its influence over time.

Limiting beliefs also distort perception. The mind selectively attends to information that confirms existing beliefs while ignoring contradictory evidence. Success may be attributed to luck, while failure is interpreted as proof of inadequacy. This confirmation bias preserves the belief and stabilizes identity, making change feel risky. Because the belief shapes interpretation, experience rarely challenges it directly.

Social feedback often amplifies limiting beliefs. Criticism, comparison, or lack of validation can reinforce internal narratives of inadequacy or unworthiness. Cultural norms and expectations may further legitimize these beliefs, making them seem rational or responsible. Over time, the belief becomes normalized, embedded in identity, and resistant to conscious challenge.

Importantly, limiting beliefs are not inherently negative. They originate as attempts to protect the individual from harm or disappointment. The problem arises when these beliefs persist beyond their usefulness. A belief that once reduced emotional risk may later restrict growth and opportunity. Because the belief feels protective, the mind resists letting it go.

Limiting beliefs also affect self-regulation. When behavior conflicts with belief, internal tension arises. To resolve this tension, individuals often abandon the behavior rather than challenge the belief. This dynamic explains why people may sabotage progress or withdraw just as success becomes possible. The belief system seeks consistency, even at the expense of desired outcomes.

Changing limiting beliefs requires more than positive thinking. Logical arguments rarely override emotionally reinforced beliefs. Change begins with awareness—recognizing the belief as a conclusion rather than a fact. This recognition creates psychological distance, reducing automatic influence. Gradual behavioral experiments that produce new emotional outcomes are essential for updating beliefs.

As new experiences accumulate, the emotional foundation of the limiting belief weakens. Alternative interpretations become possible, and identity becomes more flexible. Action no longer feels threatening because it no longer violates core assumptions about the self.

Limiting beliefs shape action by defining what feels possible. When these beliefs are examined and revised, behavioral freedom expands. Understanding this process allows individuals to move beyond self-imposed boundaries and act in ways that reflect potential rather than fear.

Reprogramming Internal Narratives

Internal narratives are the ongoing stories individuals tell themselves about who they are, how the world works, and what outcomes they can expect. These narratives are not passive reflections of reality; they actively shape perception, emotion, and behavior. Formed through experience and reinforced through repetition, internal narratives function as operating systems that guide action automatically. Reprogramming these narratives is therefore a critical step in altering behavior and expanding psychological freedom.

Internal narratives develop as the mind seeks coherence. Experiences are organized into stories that explain cause and effect, success and failure, and personal value. When similar experiences occur repeatedly, the associated interpretations become consolidated into a dominant narrative. For example, repeated struggles may be interpreted as evidence of inadequacy, while repeated reinforcement may support a narrative of competence. Once established, these narratives guide attention and expectation, influencing how new experiences are interpreted.

Language plays a central role in narrative formation. The words individuals use to describe themselves and their experiences shape cognitive and emotional response. Statements such as "I always fail" or "I am not the type of person who succeeds" are not neutral descriptions; they are narrative declarations that frame future experience. Over time, these linguistic patterns become internalized, shaping automatic thought and emotional response.

Internal narratives influence behavior by establishing identity-consistent action. People are motivated to act in ways that align with their self-story, even when that story is limiting. A narrative of incompetence encourages avoidance, while a narrative of resilience supports persistence. Because these narratives operate beneath awareness, behavior feels justified rather than constrained.

Reprogramming internal narratives begins with awareness. This involves identifying recurring self-statements and recognizing them as narratives rather than facts. Awareness creates distance between the observer and the story, weakening automatic identification. This shift does not require immediate replacement of the narrative; it requires recognition of its constructed nature.

Emotional engagement is essential in narrative change. Internal narratives are reinforced by emotional memory, not logic. New narratives must be paired with emotional experiences that contradict the old story. Small, consistent actions that produce different emotional outcomes gradually weaken existing narratives. This process requires patience, as the mind resists abrupt changes that threaten identity stability.

Behavioral alignment accelerates narrative reprogramming. When individuals act in ways that challenge old narratives, the mind must reconcile behavior with belief. Repeated action that contradicts the narrative creates cognitive dissonance, prompting reinterpretation. Over time, the narrative adjusts to accommodate new evidence.

Social context also influences narrative change. Feedback from others can either reinforce or challenge internal stories. Surrounding oneself with environments that support growth and authenticity reduces resistance to new narratives. Conversely, environments that reinforce old stories slow change.

Importantly, reprogramming internal narratives does not involve denial of past experience. It involves reframing interpretation. The goal is not to erase history but to reinterpret it through a broader lens. Experiences once seen as failure can be reclassified as learning. This reframing alters emotional association and behavioral expectation.

Narrative change is a gradual process. Old narratives rarely disappear completely; they lose dominance as new narratives gain strength. Moments of doubt or regression are part of adaptation, not failure. Persistence and consistency are key.

Internal narratives shape the boundaries of action. When these narratives are updated, behavior expands naturally. Reprogramming internal narratives allows individuals to act from choice rather than habit, creating alignment between intention, belief, and behavior.

Chapter 6

The Role of Perception and Interpretation

Human beings do not respond to the world as it objectively exists; they respond to the world as it is perceived and interpreted. Every experience passes through a mental framework shaped by past learning, emotional history, beliefs, and expectations. This framework determines what is noticed, how it is understood, and what meaning is assigned. As a result, perception does not simply reflect reality—it actively constructs it.

This chapter explores perception as a powerful psychological force that shapes behavior long before conscious decision-making begins. The mind constantly interprets sensory information, filling gaps, assigning significance, and predicting outcomes. These interpretations happen rapidly and largely outside awareness. Two individuals can encounter the same situation and respond in entirely different ways because their minds construct different versions of reality from the same input.

Cognitive filters and biases play a central role in this process. The brain prioritizes information that aligns with existing beliefs and emotional states while filtering out what feels irrelevant or threatening. This selective attention creates consistency and efficiency but also limits flexibility. Once a particular interpretation becomes habitual, it influences emotion and action automatically, often without being questioned.

Perception also functions as a behavioral compass. How a situation is perceived determines whether it invites engagement, avoidance, or neutrality. A challenge perceived as an opportunity encourages effort; the same challenge perceived as a threat triggers withdrawal. In this way, perception directs behavior by shaping emotional response and expectation before conscious choice is involved.

By understanding how perception and interpretation operate, individuals gain insight into why behavior often feels justified yet inconsistent with intention. This chapter lays the foundation for recognizing perception as a dynamic, learnable process—and a critical leverage point for changing how one experiences and responds to the world.

How Reality Is Mentally Constructed

Reality is often assumed to be a fixed, objective environment that individuals perceive directly and respond to accordingly. In practice, however, human beings do not experience reality in its raw form. What is experienced as "reality" is the product of an active mental construction process that interprets sensory input, assigns meaning, and generates emotional and behavioral responses. This process occurs continuously and largely outside conscious awareness, shaping how individuals understand the world and how they act within it.

At the most basic level, perception begins with sensory data. The eyes, ears, and other sensory systems transmit information to the brain, but this information is incomplete and ambiguous. The brain must organize and interpret it to create a coherent experience. Rather than processing every detail, the mind relies on prior knowledge, expectations, and context to fill in gaps. This predictive approach allows for efficient functioning but introduces subjectivity into perception.

Memory plays a central role in constructing reality. Past experiences provide templates that guide interpretation of present situations. When the mind encounters a familiar pattern, it quickly categorizes the experience based on stored memory. This categorization influences emotional response and expectation. A situation that resembles a past threat may be interpreted as dangerous, while one associated with success may be seen as an opportunity. The individual experiences this interpretation as reality rather than as a memory-driven inference.

Emotions further shape mental construction by signaling significance. Emotional states bias attention, determining which aspects of a situation are highlighted and which are ignored. Anxiety amplifies perceived threat, while positive emotion broadens perception and increases openness. These emotional influences operate rapidly, shaping interpretation before conscious reasoning can intervene. As a result, emotional state at the time of perception can alter the constructed reality.

Beliefs function as interpretive frameworks that organize perception. Core beliefs about the self, others, and the world act as lenses through which information is filtered. A belief such as "people are untrustworthy" predisposes the mind to interpret ambiguous behavior as hostile.

Conversely, a belief in personal competence may lead to interpreting challenges as manageable. These belief-driven interpretations feel natural and obvious, masking their constructed nature.

Language also contributes to reality construction. The words used to label experiences influence how they are understood and remembered. Describing an event as a failure versus a learning experience alters emotional response and future behavior. Language does not merely describe reality; it shapes the meaning assigned to experience, reinforcing particular interpretations over others.

Social context further influences mental construction. Cultural norms, shared narratives, and collective beliefs provide interpretive frameworks that shape individual perception. From early development, individuals learn how to interpret behavior, emotion, and events based on social feedback. These shared interpretations become internalized, guiding perception even in private experience.

Importantly, the brain prioritizes coherence over accuracy. It seeks interpretations that maintain internal consistency, even if they distort reality. When new information conflicts with existing beliefs or expectations, it is often minimized, reinterpreted, or ignored. This cognitive tendency stabilizes perception but reduces openness to change. The resulting reality feels stable and predictable, reinforcing existing behavioral patterns.

Stress and cognitive load intensify reliance on mental construction. Under pressure, the brain relies more heavily on familiar interpretations and less on reflective analysis. This explains why perception becomes more rigid during times of stress, leading to heightened reactivity and reduced behavioral flexibility.

Understanding that reality is mentally constructed does not imply that experience is illusory or arbitrary. It highlights the role of interpretation in shaping experience. The external world provides stimuli, but the meaning and significance of those stimuli are created internally. Recognizing this distinction empowers individuals to question automatic interpretations and explore alternative perspectives.

By becoming aware of the construction process, individuals gain the ability to intervene. They can examine the assumptions, memories, and emotions shaping perception. This awareness creates space for reinterpretation, allowing behavior to shift accordingly.

Reality, as experienced, is not simply discovered—it is assembled. Understanding how this assembly occurs reveals why people can live in different psychological worlds while sharing the same environment. It also reveals perception as a powerful leverage point for intentional change in thought, emotion, and action.

Cognitive Filters and Biases

Human perception is not a neutral recording of reality. The mind relies on cognitive filters and biases to manage overwhelming amounts of information and to make rapid judgments. These mental shortcuts are adaptive, allowing individuals to function efficiently in complex environments. However, they also distort perception, influencing interpretation, emotion, and behavior in systematic ways. Understanding these filters and biases is essential for recognizing why people often see the same situation differently and act in predictable yet flawed patterns.

Cognitive filters operate by selecting which information enters conscious awareness and how it is interpreted. Attention is limited, so the brain prioritizes information that appears relevant to survival, goals, and identity. This prioritization is influenced by emotional state, past experience, and belief systems. Information that aligns with existing beliefs is more likely to be noticed and accepted, while contradictory information is often filtered out or discounted. This selective attention creates a stable internal reality but reduces openness to alternative interpretations.

Biases are the consistent tendencies that shape how information is processed once it has passed through these filters. One of the most influential biases is confirmation bias—the tendency to seek, interpret, and remember information that confirms existing beliefs. This bias reinforces internal narratives and belief systems, making change difficult. Even neutral events are interpreted in ways that support established assumptions, giving the impression that beliefs are repeatedly validated by reality.

Another common bias is negativity bias, which causes negative information to carry greater psychological weight than positive information. From an evolutionary perspective, prioritizing threat detection increased survival. In modern contexts, however, this bias can lead to exaggerated perceptions of risk, criticism, or failure. Negative experiences are remembered more vividly and influence future behavior more strongly than positive ones, shaping avoidance and self-doubt.

Availability bias also plays a role in perception and decision-making. The mind assesses the likelihood of events based on how easily examples come to mind. Emotionally charged or recent experiences are more accessible, leading to distorted judgments about frequency and risk. A single negative incident can disproportionately influence behavior if it is easily recalled, even when it is statistically rare.

Cognitive filters are also shaped by identity. Information that threatens self-concept is more likely to be dismissed or rationalized. This self-serving bias preserves psychological stability by protecting identity from challenge. While this can reduce emotional distress in the short term, it limits growth by preventing honest self-assessment.

Social and cultural influences further reinforce cognitive biases. Shared narratives and group norms shape collective filters, guiding interpretation of events in ways that maintain group cohesion. These influences can lead to conformity and resistance to information that challenges group beliefs. In such contexts, biases are reinforced not only internally but socially.

Stress and emotional arousal intensify reliance on cognitive filters and biases. Under pressure, the brain prioritizes speed over accuracy, defaulting to familiar interpretations. This results in more rigid thinking, reduced nuance, and increased reactivity. Bias-driven perception becomes more pronounced, shaping behavior in automatic ways.

Importantly, cognitive filters and biases are not signs of weakness or irrationality. They are natural features of human cognition. Problems arise when individuals are unaware of their influence and mistake filtered perception for objective reality. This unawareness leads to repetitive behavioral patterns and conflict between intention and action.

Awareness is the first step in mitigating the impact of biases. By recognizing that perception is filtered, individuals can question automatic interpretations and seek alternative perspectives. This does not eliminate biases but reduces their control over behavior. Reflection, feedback, and exposure to diverse viewpoints help expand perceptual range.

Cognitive filters and biases shape how reality is experienced and how decisions are made. When left unexamined, they reinforce limiting beliefs and habitual behavior. When understood, they become leverage points for greater clarity, flexibility, and intentional action.

Perception as a Behavioral Compass

Perception functions as an internal compass that guides behavior by determining how situations are understood and what actions feel appropriate. Long before conscious decision-making begins, perception assigns meaning, evaluates significance, and predicts outcomes. These interpretations direct behavior automatically, shaping responses that feel logical and justified. In this way, perception does not merely inform action—it actively steers it.

At the core of this process is the link between perception and emotional response. How a situation is perceived determines whether it is experienced as safe or threatening, rewarding or pointless. A task perceived as an opportunity generates engagement and effort. The same task perceived as a threat triggers avoidance or resistance. Emotion follows perception, and behavior follows emotion. This sequence occurs rapidly and largely outside awareness, making perception a powerful determinant of action.

Perception also influences motivation by shaping expectancy. If the mind perceives success as likely, effort increases. If failure is perceived as inevitable, motivation collapses. These expectancies are not objective assessments; they are constructed from past experience, belief, and emotional memory. Because expectancy influences persistence, perception quietly determines whether action is sustained or abandoned.

Identity further anchors perception as a behavioral guide. Individuals perceive situations in ways that align with their self-concept. A person who identifies as competent may interpret challenges as tests of skill, while someone who identifies as inadequate may see the same challenges as confirmation of limitation. These identity-based perceptions guide action by reinforcing consistency between belief and behavior.

Social perception plays a critical role as well. How individuals believe they are seen by others influences behavior through anticipation of approval or rejection. Situations perceived as socially risky may be avoided, even when personally meaningful. Conversely, environments perceived as supportive encourage expression and engagement. These social perceptions operate continuously, shaping behavior in subtle ways.

Perception also affects decision speed and flexibility. When situations are perceived as familiar, action is automatic and rapid. When situations are perceived as uncertain or threatening, hesitation increases. Under stress, perception becomes more rigid, narrowing options and reinforcing habitual responses. This rigidity can trap individuals in patterns that feel unavoidable.

Importantly, perception is learned rather than fixed. Repeated interpretations become habits, forming perceptual defaults that guide behavior consistently. These defaults feel natural, masking their constructed nature. Without awareness, individuals mistake perception for reality and act accordingly.

Changing behavior therefore requires changing perception. This does not mean denying reality but reinterpreting meaning. When individuals learn to question automatic perceptions and explore alternative interpretations, emotional response shifts. As emotion shifts, behavior follows. This process requires awareness, emotional regulation, and exposure to new experiences that challenge existing perceptual patterns.

Perception as a behavioral compass explains why behavior often persists despite conscious intention. The mind acts in alignment with perceived reality, not abstract goals. When perception aligns with purpose, action feels effortless. When perception conflicts with intention, action becomes inconsistent.

Ultimately, behavior follows the direction set by perception. By understanding perception as an active guide rather than a passive reflection, individuals gain leverage over action. Adjusting the compass changes the course, allowing behavior to align more closely with intention, values, and long-term goals.

Chapter 7

Social Influence and Psychological Pressure

Human behavior does not develop in isolation. From the earliest stages of life, individuals are shaped by social environments that teach what is acceptable, valued, and expected. These influences operate continuously, guiding action through subtle cues and overt pressure. Much of what people believe to be personal choice is, in fact, the result of social conditioning that has been internalized over time.

This chapter examines how society and culture shape behavior through psychological pressure. Social norms define boundaries of behavior, signaling which actions lead to acceptance and which risk rejection. Over time, these external signals become internal standards that guide behavior even when no one is watching. This internalization explains why individuals often conform automatically, without consciously evaluating whether conformity aligns with personal values.

Approval and rejection are powerful emotional forces in social contexts. The desire for belonging and the fear of exclusion influence behavior more strongly than logic or self-interest. Many actions are driven not by intrinsic motivation, but by the anticipation of social response. Even subtle cues—such as tone, facial expression, or silence—can shape behavior by signaling approval or disapproval.

The chapter also explores the psychology of authority and obedience. Hierarchies and power structures shape perception and behavior by assigning legitimacy to certain voices. When authority is perceived as legitimate, individuals often comply automatically, suspending personal judgment. This tendency is not a flaw in character but a deeply ingrained psychological response designed to maintain social order.

By examining conditioning, conformity, and obedience, this chapter reveals how social forces influence behavior beneath awareness. Understanding these mechanisms allows individuals to distinguish between authentic choice and conditioned response. Awareness of social pressure is a critical step toward acting with intention rather than reflex in a socially structured world.

Conditioning Through Society and Culture

Human behavior is shaped not only by individual experience but by the social and cultural systems in which individuals are embedded. From birth, people are conditioned through repeated exposure to norms, values, expectations, and narratives that define what is acceptable and meaningful. This conditioning does not rely on explicit instruction alone; it operates through subtle reinforcement, observation, and emotional feedback. Over time, social and cultural influences become internalized, guiding behavior automatically and often invisibly.

Cultural conditioning begins early in life, when individuals are highly receptive to external cues. Family structures, educational systems, religious practices, and media all transmit messages about identity, success, morality, and belonging. These messages shape foundational beliefs about how one should behave and what outcomes are desirable. Because these lessons are learned implicitly, they are rarely questioned. They form the backdrop against which personal choices are made.

Social reinforcement plays a central role in conditioning. Behaviors that receive approval are reinforced, while those that provoke disapproval or punishment are discouraged. This reinforcement is not always explicit. Subtle cues such as praise, attention, withdrawal, or comparison communicate powerful signals. Over time, individuals learn to anticipate social responses and adjust behavior accordingly. This anticipation becomes internalized, allowing social norms to guide behavior even in the absence of immediate feedback.

Observation is another powerful mechanism of conditioning. Individuals learn not only from direct experience but by observing the behavior of others and its consequences. Social models—parents, peers, authority figures, and cultural icons—demonstrate what behaviors lead to acceptance, success, or rejection. These observed patterns inform behavioral expectations and influence imitation. Through repeated observation, individuals adopt behaviors that align with social norms without conscious decision.

Language and narrative further reinforce cultural conditioning. Shared stories, metaphors, and labels shape how individuals interpret experience. Cultural narratives define roles, values, and expectations, influencing identity and aspiration. When individuals internalize these narratives, they begin to evaluate themselves and others through culturally defined standards. This narrative conditioning shapes motivation and self-concept, often limiting perceived options.

Cultural conditioning also operates through structure and routine. Institutions such as schools, workplaces, and governments organize behavior through rules, schedules, and hierarchies. These structures shape habits and expectations, reinforcing compliance and conformity. Over time, institutional norms become personal norms, guiding behavior automatically.

Emotional conditioning is particularly powerful. Acceptance generates positive emotion, while rejection generates discomfort. Because belonging is a fundamental human need, individuals learn to avoid behaviors that risk social exclusion. This avoidance often occurs without conscious awareness, shaping behavior in subtle ways. Actions that align with group norms feel safe, while deviation feels risky.

Importantly, cultural conditioning is not inherently harmful. It provides order, predictability, and shared meaning. However, it can also suppress individuality and critical thinking when norms are rigid or misaligned with personal values. When conditioning remains unexamined, individuals may conform automatically, mistaking learned behavior for personal choice.

Change requires awareness of conditioning influences. By recognizing how social and cultural systems shape behavior, individuals can evaluate whether those influences align with their values and goals. This awareness creates space for intentional choice rather than reflexive conformity.

Conditioning through society and culture demonstrates that behavior is not solely a product of individual psychology. It is the outcome of continuous interaction with social environments. Understanding this process allows individuals to navigate social pressure with greater autonomy, acting with intention rather than unconscious compliance.

Approval, Rejection, and Conformity

Human beings are inherently social creatures, wired to seek connection, acceptance, and belonging. From an early age, behavior is shaped by the emotional consequences of approval and rejection. These social responses function as powerful psychological signals that guide action, often more forcefully than logic or personal preference. Over time, the desire for approval and the fear of rejection become internal regulators of behavior, driving conformity in ways that feel natural rather than imposed.

Approval operates as a form of emotional reward. Positive feedback, recognition, and inclusion generate feelings of safety and belonging. When a behavior leads to approval, it is reinforced and more likely to be repeated. This reinforcement does not require conscious awareness; the emotional satisfaction associated with acceptance is enough to shape future action. Over time, individuals learn which behaviors align with group expectations and adjust accordingly.

Rejection functions as the opposing force, signaling social threat. Disapproval, exclusion, or indifference trigger emotional discomfort and stress responses. These reactions are rooted in survival mechanisms, as social exclusion historically posed serious risks. Even in modern contexts, the emotional impact of rejection remains powerful. As a result, individuals often avoid behaviors that might provoke disapproval, even when those behaviors align with personal values or goals.

Conformity emerges from the interplay of approval and rejection. To maintain social safety, individuals adapt their behavior to align with perceived norms. This adaptation often occurs unconsciously, guided by subtle cues rather than explicit instruction. Tone of voice, facial expression, and group dynamics signal what is acceptable, shaping behavior in real time.

Importantly, conformity does not require agreement. Individuals may privately disagree with group norms while publicly complying to avoid rejection. This discrepancy between internal belief and external behavior can create psychological tension, yet conformity persists because the emotional cost of deviation feels greater than the cost of compliance.

Approval and rejection also influence self-concept. Repeated feedback shapes beliefs about worth and competence. When approval is conditional, individuals may tie self-esteem to external validation, increasing sensitivity to social cues. This dependency strengthens conformity by making approval essential to emotional stability.

Social environments amplify these dynamics. Group settings increase pressure to conform, particularly when norms are unclear or authority is present. Uncertainty heightens reliance on social cues, making individuals more susceptible to influence. In such contexts, conformity feels protective rather than restrictive.

Importantly, conformity is not inherently negative. It supports social cohesion, cooperation, and shared norms. However, when conformity suppresses authenticity or critical thinking, it limits personal agency. Individuals may act against their own values to preserve belonging, often without recognizing the influence at work.

Reducing the impact of approval-driven behavior requires awareness and emotional regulation. Recognizing the emotional triggers associated with approval and rejection allows individuals to pause before reacting. Developing internal sources of validation reduces dependence on external feedback, increasing behavioral autonomy.

Approval, rejection, and conformity illustrate how deeply social forces shape action. Behavior is often guided not by conscious choice but by the emotional pull of belonging. Understanding this dynamic allows individuals to navigate social influence with greater intention, choosing when to conform and when to act independently.

The Psychology of Authority and Obedience

Authority exerts a powerful influence over human behavior, often shaping action more strongly than personal values or independent judgment. Throughout history and across cultures, individuals have demonstrated a consistent tendency to defer to perceived authority figures, complying with instructions even when those instructions conflict with personal beliefs. This tendency is not simply a matter of personality or morality; it is rooted in fundamental psychological processes that govern social order and survival.

From early development, individuals are conditioned to recognize and respond to authority. Parents, teachers, and institutional figures provide structure and guidance, establishing patterns of obedience that facilitate learning and coordination. Compliance is often rewarded with approval, while resistance may be met with punishment or disapproval. Over time, these experiences teach individuals that obedience to authority is associated with safety and acceptance.

Authority functions as a cognitive shortcut. In complex environments, evaluating every instruction independently would be cognitively demanding and potentially risky. Deferring to authority reduces uncertainty by transferring responsibility for decision-making to a figure perceived as knowledgeable or legitimate. This transfer of responsibility lowers psychological burden and increases compliance, particularly under conditions of stress or ambiguity.

Perceived legitimacy is central to authority's influence. Individuals are more likely to obey when authority is associated with expertise, status, or institutional backing. Symbols such as uniforms, titles, or formal settings reinforce legitimacy, triggering automatic compliance. These cues activate learned associations, prompting obedience without conscious evaluation of the command itself.

Obedience is further reinforced by social context. When others comply, conformity pressures amplify authority's influence. Resistance becomes socially risky, increasing the emotional cost of disobedience. In group settings, responsibility is diffused, reducing personal accountability and making compliance easier. These dynamics explain why individuals may engage in actions they would not choose independently.

Emotional factors also play a role. Fear of punishment, desire for approval, and anxiety about consequences strengthen obedience. Even mild authority can elicit compliance if emotional stakes are perceived as high. Conversely, emotional detachment or moral disengagement can reduce resistance, allowing individuals to comply without fully processing the implications of their actions.

Importantly, obedience does not require explicit coercion. Subtle authority cues can guide behavior through expectation and habit. Individuals often anticipate what authority wants and adjust behavior preemptively. This anticipatory obedience operates beneath awareness, shaping action even in the absence of direct instruction.

Authority can also shape belief. Repeated compliance can lead to internalization, where individuals adopt the values or perspectives of authority figures. This internalization reduces cognitive dissonance and stabilizes identity. Over time, obedience becomes self-reinforcing, as beliefs align with behavior.

While authority supports social coordination, it also poses risks when unchecked. Automatic obedience can suppress critical thinking and moral judgment. Individuals may prioritize compliance over conscience, particularly in hierarchical systems that discourage questioning. Recognizing this risk is essential for maintaining ethical agency.

Reducing blind obedience requires awareness and personal responsibility. When individuals recognize authority's psychological influence, they can re-engage judgment and evaluate commands more consciously. Developing internal standards and moral clarity strengthens resistance to inappropriate authority.

The psychology of authority and obedience reveals that behavior is shaped not only by personal intention but by social structure. Understanding this influence allows individuals to navigate authority with discernment, balancing cooperation with autonomy.

Chapter 8

The Conflict Between Logic and Impulse

Human behavior is often described as a product of reasoned choice, yet much of daily action is driven by impulse. People routinely act in ways that contradict their knowledge, intentions, and long-term goals. This internal conflict between logic and impulse is not a failure of intelligence or character; it is a reflection of how the human mind is structured. Different psychological systems compete for control, each operating according to its own priorities and timelines.

This chapter explores the tension between rational thought and emotional urge. Rational thinking is deliberate, reflective, and future-oriented. It weighs consequences and considers long-term outcomes. Impulse, by contrast, is immediate and emotionally driven. It seeks relief, pleasure, or safety in the present moment. When these systems align, action feels effortless. When they conflict, behavior becomes inconsistent and often regrettable.

Impulse control and self-regulation depend on more than awareness. Stress, fatigue, emotional arousal, and environmental cues all weaken rational influence and strengthen impulse-driven behavior. Under such conditions, the mind prioritizes speed and emotional regulation over deliberation. This explains why people often make choices they later question, especially under pressure.

The chapter also examines why acting against better judgment feels so frustrating. Knowledge alone does not govern behavior; emotional urgency often overrides logic. Impulse-driven actions provide immediate emotional payoff, even when they undermine long-term goals. Understanding this dynamic shifts the focus from self-blame to system awareness.

By examining the interaction between logic and impulse, this chapter reveals why self-control fluctuates and how it can be strengthened. Recognizing the structural nature of this conflict is essential for developing realistic strategies for consistent, intentional action.

Rational Thought vs. Emotional Urge

Human decision-making is often portrayed as a rational process guided by careful analysis and conscious choice. In practice, however, rational thought frequently competes with emotional urge for control over behavior. This competition is not a flaw in human nature but a consequence of how the mind is organized. Different psychological systems evolved to serve different functions, and they operate according to different rules. Understanding this dynamic is essential for explaining why people so often act against their own stated intentions.

Rational thought is deliberate and reflective. It relies on conscious awareness, language, and logical evaluation. This system considers future consequences, weighs alternatives, and integrates abstract goals. It allows individuals to plan, delay gratification, and align action with long-term values. However, rational processing is slow and cognitively demanding. It requires attention and mental energy, both of which are limited resources.

Emotional urge operates differently. It is fast, automatic, and rooted in survival-oriented systems. Emotional urges arise from the brain's evaluation of immediate relevance—what feels good, bad, threatening, or relieving in the present moment. These urges mobilize action quickly, often before conscious reasoning has time to intervene. From an evolutionary perspective, speed mattered more than accuracy. Immediate response increased survival, even if it occasionally produced suboptimal outcomes.

The conflict between these systems becomes evident in situations involving temptation, stress, or uncertainty. Rational thought may identify a course of action that supports long-term goals, while emotional urge pushes toward immediate relief or reward. For example, a person may understand the benefits of healthy behavior yet choose comfort in moments of emotional distress. The emotional system prioritizes regulation of feeling over abstract outcomes.

Emotional urges gain strength through repetition and reinforcement. Behaviors that successfully reduce discomfort or produce pleasure are reinforced emotionally, making similar urges more likely in the future. Over time, these emotional patterns become habitual, activating automatically in response to cues. Rational thought must then compete not only with momentary urge but with established emotional-behavioral loops.

Stress and fatigue shift the balance toward emotional urge. When cognitive resources are depleted, rational control weakens. The brain defaults to faster, less demanding systems. This explains why impulse control is most difficult under pressure. Emotional urges feel more compelling, and rational considerations lose influence. The resulting behavior often feels inevitable rather than chosen.

Importantly, rational thought does not eliminate emotional urge. Attempts to suppress emotion through logic alone often fail because they ignore the underlying emotional need. Emotional urges are signals, not enemies. They communicate unmet needs, perceived threats, or desired rewards. When these signals are ignored or invalidated, they intensify rather than disappear.

Effective self-regulation involves integrating rational thought and emotional awareness. When individuals acknowledge emotional urges without acting on them immediately, they create space for rational evaluation. This pause allows both systems to contribute to the decision. Emotional information can be considered alongside long-term goals rather than overriding them.

Identity also influences the balance between logic and impulse. Individuals who see themselves as disciplined or self-regulated are more likely to engage rational control. Conversely, those who identify as impulsive may unconsciously reinforce emotional dominance. Identity shapes expectation, which in turn influences behavior.

The conflict between rational thought and emotional urge is not a battle to be won but a dynamic to be managed. Rational thought provides direction and coherence, while emotional urge provides energy and immediacy. When these systems are aligned, action feels purposeful and sustainable. When they are misaligned, behavior becomes inconsistent and frustrating.

Understanding this conflict reframes self-control as a skill rather than a trait. It highlights the importance of context, emotional regulation, and energy management. By recognizing when emotional urges are driving behavior, individuals can intervene consciously, strengthening rational influence without denying emotional reality.

Ultimately, behavior reflects the system that is most active in the moment. Developing awareness of the interplay between rational thought and emotional urge allows individuals to act with greater intention, balancing immediate feeling with long-term purpose.

Impulse Control and Self-Regulation

Impulse control and self-regulation are often misunderstood as traits that some people naturally possess and others lack. In reality, they are dynamic psychological capacities shaped by biology, learning, emotional state, and environment. Self-regulation is not the absence of impulse; it is the ability to manage impulses in a way that aligns behavior with long-term goals and values. Understanding how impulse control functions reveals why it fluctuates and how it can be strengthened.

Impulses arise from fast, emotionally driven systems designed to respond immediately to perceived needs or threats. These systems prioritize short-term relief, pleasure, or safety. Self-regulation, by contrast, relies on slower, effortful processes that evaluate consequences and delay gratification. Because these systems operate differently, impulse control requires active coordination rather than suppression.

One of the most important factors influencing self-regulation is emotional state. Strong emotions amplify impulses by increasing urgency. Anxiety drives avoidance, desire drives pursuit, and frustration drives escape. When emotional intensity is high, impulses feel compelling and difficult to resist. This is why self-regulation often fails during moments of stress, excitement, or emotional exhaustion. The emotional system temporarily dominates, reducing access to reflective control.

Cognitive resources also play a critical role. Self-regulation depends on attention, working memory, and mental energy. When these resources are depleted through fatigue, multitasking, or prolonged stress, impulse control weakens. The brain defaults to automatic responses that require less effort. This phenomenon explains why individuals may regulate behavior effectively in one context and struggle in another.

Habits further influence impulse control. Repeated impulse-driven behaviors become automated, reducing the need for conscious choice. Over time, cues alone can trigger impulsive responses. In such cases, self-regulation requires interrupting established patterns rather than resisting a single urge. Without addressing the habitual structure, attempts at control are fragile and inconsistent.

Environment significantly affects self-regulation. Cues, accessibility, and social context shape impulse strength. Environments that reduce temptation or support intentional behavior lower the demand for self-control. Conversely, environments saturated with triggers require constant effort, increasing the likelihood of failure. Effective self-regulation often involves modifying surroundings rather than relying solely on internal restraint.

Importantly, impulse control is not about rigid discipline. Excessive suppression of impulse can backfire, increasing emotional tension and rebound behavior. Sustainable self-regulation involves acknowledging impulses without immediately acting on them. This acknowledgment reduces urgency and allows space for choice. Emotional awareness, rather than denial, strengthens regulation.

Meaning and identity also support self-regulation. When behavior aligns with personal values and self-concept, regulation feels purposeful rather than restrictive. A clear sense of purpose increases tolerance for discomfort, making delayed gratification more sustainable. Identity-based motivation stabilizes self-regulation when emotional states fluctuate.

Skill development is central to improving impulse control. Techniques such as pausing, reframing, and redirecting attention increase regulatory capacity. Repeated practice strengthens neural pathways associated with regulation, making self-control more accessible over time. Like any skill, self-regulation improves with consistent use.

Understanding impulse control reframes failure as feedback rather than deficiency. Lapses reveal conditions under which regulation is weakened, providing information for adjustment. By addressing emotional triggers, environmental cues, and cognitive load, individuals can design systems that support consistent behavior.

Impulse control and self-regulation are not about perfection. They are about flexibility—the ability to respond intentionally rather than reflexively. When regulation is understood as a dynamic process shaped by multiple factors, it becomes something that can be cultivated rather than demanded.

Why We Act Against Better Judgment

Acting against better judgment is one of the most perplexing aspects of human behavior. People often know what they should do, understand the consequences of their actions, and genuinely intend to act wisely—yet they do the opposite. This contradiction is not a failure of intelligence or morality. It is the result of competing psychological systems operating under different priorities, speeds, and sources of motivation.

One of the primary reasons people act against better judgment is the dominance of immediate emotional needs over abstract reasoning. Better judgment is typically future-oriented, weighing long-term outcomes and delayed rewards. Emotional systems, by contrast, are present-focused. They prioritize relief, comfort, pleasure, or safety in the moment. When emotional urgency is high, it eclipses rational evaluation. The mind chooses what feels manageable now over what is beneficial later.

Stress intensifies this imbalance. Under stress, cognitive resources narrow, and the brain shifts into efficiency mode. Reflective thinking becomes more difficult, while automatic responses become more accessible. In these conditions, behavior is guided by habit, emotion, and learned shortcuts rather than deliberate judgment. This explains why people often regret decisions made under pressure—they were made in a different psychological state than the one evaluating them afterward.

Another key factor is emotional reinforcement. Actions that provide immediate emotional payoff—such as relief from anxiety, distraction from discomfort, or a sense of control—are reinforced, even if they undermine long-term goals. The brain learns that these actions work emotionally, strengthening the impulse to repeat them. Over time, this reinforcement creates behavioral loops that operate independently of conscious intention.

Cognitive dissonance also contributes to acting against better judgment. When behavior conflicts with values or knowledge, discomfort arises. Rather than changing behavior, the mind often resolves this tension by justifying the action. Rationalizations such as "just this once" or "it won't matter" reduce discomfort and allow the behavior to continue. This process preserves self-image while enabling repeated violations of better judgment.

Identity plays a subtle but powerful role. People act in ways that align with their self-concept, even when that self-concept is limiting. A person who unconsciously identifies as impulsive or inconsistent may act accordingly, reinforcing the identity through behavior. In such cases, acting against better judgment maintains internal consistency, which the mind prioritizes over improvement.

Environmental cues further weaken judgment. Situations saturated with triggers increase the likelihood of impulsive action. Accessibility, social pressure, and familiarity reduce the psychological distance between urge and action. Without structural support, better judgment must compete constantly with immediate cues, a competition it often loses.

Importantly, better judgment itself is fragile. It depends on attention, emotional balance, and energy. When these resources are depleted, judgment loses influence. This explains why people often make wise decisions in calm moments and poor ones when tired, hungry, or overwhelmed. The judgment did not disappear; the conditions supporting it did.

Understanding why people act against better judgment shifts the narrative from self-blame to system awareness. Behavior reflects the strongest influence present in the moment, not the best reasoning available in theory. Change therefore requires strengthening the conditions that support judgment—emotional regulation, habit redesign, environmental structure, and identity alignment.

Acting against better judgment is not evidence of weakness. It is evidence of how human behavior is shaped by timing, emotion, and context. When these factors are understood and addressed, judgment gains practical influence, and action becomes more consistent with intention.

Chapter 9

Identity, Self-Image, and Action

Human behavior is deeply tied to identity—the internal sense of who one is and how one fits into the world. Identity is not merely a label or a collection of traits; it is an organizing framework that shapes perception, motivation, and action. People tend to act in ways that are consistent with their self-image, often without conscious awareness. When behavior aligns with identity, action feels natural and sustainable. When it conflicts, resistance and discomfort arise.

This chapter explores identity as a powerful driver of behavior. Self-concept influences what individuals believe they are capable of, what goals feel attainable, and what actions feel appropriate. A person who sees themselves as disciplined is more likely to engage in consistent effort, while someone who identifies as unreliable may unconsciously reinforce that narrative through behavior. Identity acts as an internal reference point, guiding action before conscious reasoning is engaged.

The psychological cost of inconsistency is a key theme. When actions contradict self-image, internal tension emerges. To resolve this tension, individuals often adjust behavior or reinterpret experience in ways that restore coherence. This process explains why people may abandon positive changes that threaten existing identity, even when the changes are desired.

The chapter also examines how identity can be intentionally reshaped to support new behavior. Reinventing identity does not require denying the past; it involves updating self-concept through awareness, experience, and repetition. When behavior is framed as an expression of a chosen identity, motivation strengthens and consistency increases.

By understanding the relationship between identity and action, individuals gain access to a deeper level of change. Behavior shifts not through force, but through alignment with who one believes they are becoming.

Acting in Alignment With Self-Concept

Self-concept is the internal model individuals hold of who they are—their traits, abilities, values, and roles. This model operates as a powerful psychological organizer, guiding perception and behavior long before conscious decision-making takes place. People do not act solely based on what they want or what they know; they act in ways that feel consistent with their self-concept. When behavior aligns with this internal model, action feels natural and sustainable. When it does not, resistance emerges, often without conscious awareness.

At its core, self-concept functions as a standard for behavioral consistency. The mind seeks coherence between identity and action because consistency provides psychological stability. Acting in alignment with self-concept reduces internal tension and reinforces a sense of predictability and control. As a result, individuals are drawn toward behaviors that confirm their identity and away from those that threaten it. This attraction and avoidance occur automatically, shaping action even when the behavior conflicts with stated goals.

Self-concept is formed through accumulated experience and interpretation. Repeated feedback from the environment—successes, failures, praise, criticism—contributes to beliefs about competence, worth, and capability. Over time, these beliefs consolidate into identity statements such as "I am disciplined," "I am creative," or "I am not good at this." Once internalized, these statements act as behavioral guidelines rather than mere descriptions.

Acting in alignment with self-concept explains why certain behaviors feel effortless while others require constant effort. A person who identifies as health-conscious may naturally choose behaviors that support well-being without relying heavily on self-control. In contrast, the same behaviors may feel forced and fragile for someone whose identity does not include that trait. The difference lies not in motivation, but in alignment.

This alignment also explains resistance to change. When new behaviors challenge existing self-concept, they generate psychological discomfort. The mind interprets the behavior as inconsistent with identity, triggering doubt, hesitation, or self-sabotage. Even positive changes can be rejected if they threaten the coherence of self-image. This is why individuals may abandon progress just as it begins to succeed—the behavior no longer fits the internal story.

Self-concept influences not only action but interpretation of outcomes. Success may be dismissed as luck if it contradicts identity, while failure may be exaggerated as confirmation of limitation. This selective interpretation preserves identity by reinforcing existing beliefs. Over time, behavior and interpretation work together to stabilize self-concept, making it resistant to change.

Social context reinforces identity alignment. Others respond to individuals based on perceived identity, providing feedback that confirms or challenges self-concept. When social feedback aligns with internal beliefs, identity strengthens. When it conflicts, individuals may discount or resist it to preserve internal coherence. This dynamic further explains why acting differently can feel socially risky as well as internally uncomfortable.

Importantly, self-concept is not fixed. It is maintained through repetition and can be updated through experience. Acting in alignment with a desired identity—rather than a current one—is a powerful mechanism for change. When individuals frame behavior as an expression of who they are becoming, rather than a departure from who they are, resistance decreases. The mind begins to reinterpret actions as identity-consistent rather than identity-threatening.

Small, consistent actions are especially effective in reshaping self-concept. Each repetition provides evidence that supports a new identity narrative. Over time, the accumulation of evidence shifts belief, making new behaviors feel natural. Identity changes not through affirmation alone, but through experience interpreted consistently.

Acting in alignment with self-concept highlights why behavior change must address identity, not just habits or goals. When identity and behavior are aligned, action requires less effort and persists under pressure. When they are misaligned, progress remains fragile.

Understanding this relationship allows individuals to work with the mind rather than against it. By consciously choosing identity-aligned actions and interpreting them as evidence of growth, behavior becomes a reflection of self-concept rather than a constant struggle against it.

The Psychological Cost of Inconsistency

Inconsistency between belief, intention, and action carries a significant psychological cost. While occasional lapses are part of being human, persistent inconsistency creates internal tension that affects emotional well-being, self-trust, and behavioral stability. This tension arises because the mind seeks coherence. When actions contradict self-concept or stated values, the psyche must resolve the conflict in some way. How this conflict is resolved often determines whether growth continues or stalls.

At the center of this cost is cognitive dissonance—the discomfort experienced when behavior conflicts with beliefs or identity. The mind experiences inconsistency as a threat to psychological order. To reduce discomfort, it seeks resolution. This resolution can take the form of behavior change, belief adjustment, or rationalization. When changing behavior feels difficult, the mind often chooses the path of least resistance: altering interpretation rather than action.

Rationalization temporarily reduces discomfort but carries long-term consequences. By justifying inconsistent behavior—"this situation is different," "it doesn't really matter," or "I'll do better later"—individuals protect self-image in the moment. However, repeated rationalization weakens the credibility of internal standards. Over time, the mind learns that commitments are flexible and intentions are negotiable. This erosion of internal authority reduces motivation and self-regulation.

Inconsistency also undermines self-trust. When individuals repeatedly fail to act in accordance with their intentions, they begin to doubt their reliability. This doubt is not always conscious, but it influences future behavior. Goals feel less compelling because past experience suggests follow-through is unlikely. As self-trust declines, effort feels risky and emotionally costly, increasing avoidance and hesitation.

Emotionally, inconsistency generates guilt, shame, and frustration. These emotions are not simply reactions to failure; they reflect the internal awareness that actions are misaligned with values or identity. When unaddressed, these emotions accumulate, creating a background of self-criticism that further impairs motivation. Ironically, the emotional burden of inconsistency often drives additional inconsistent behavior as individuals seek relief from discomfort.

Behaviorally, inconsistency destabilizes habits and routines. Consistency allows behaviors to become automatic, reducing cognitive effort. Inconsistency interrupts this process, keeping behavior effortful and fragile. Each deviation resets progress, requiring renewed energy to restart. This stop-and-start pattern increases fatigue and reduces persistence.

Social consequences also contribute to psychological cost. When actions are inconsistent, others may perceive unreliability, which can affect trust and feedback. External doubt often mirrors internal doubt, reinforcing negative self-concept. Even when inconsistency is not visible to others, the anticipation of judgment can increase stress and reduce authenticity.

Importantly, inconsistency does not indicate lack of character. It often reflects misalignment between goals, identity, emotional readiness, and environment. When individuals attempt change that conflicts with self-concept or lacks adequate support, inconsistency is a predictable outcome. Treating inconsistency as a moral failure intensifies its psychological cost.

Reducing this cost begins with reframing inconsistency as information rather than evidence of inadequacy. Each inconsistency reveals something about unmet needs, conflicting beliefs, or environmental obstacles. When these factors are addressed, alignment becomes more attainable.

Consistency strengthens identity and emotional stability. When actions reliably reflect intention, self-trust grows. This trust reduces internal friction, making future action easier. Over time, consistency becomes self-reinforcing, not because of discipline alone, but because alignment reduces psychological strain.

Understanding the psychological cost of inconsistency highlights why sustainable change requires alignment rather than pressure. When identity, intention, and environment support behavior, consistency emerges naturally. When they do not, inconsistency persists, carrying emotional and cognitive costs that compound over time. Recognizing and addressing this dynamic is essential for lasting behavioral change.

Reinventing Identity to Change Behavior

Lasting behavior change rarely succeeds through effort alone. While discipline and strategy matter, they are fragile when they conflict with identity. Identity is the psychological framework through which individuals understand who they are, how they behave, and what actions feel natural or appropriate. To change behavior in a durable way, identity itself must evolve. Reinventing identity is not about pretending to be someone else; it is about updating the internal narrative that governs action.

Identity functions as a behavioral blueprint. People consistently act in ways that confirm their self-image because coherence provides psychological stability. When behavior aligns with identity, action feels authentic and requires less effort. When it conflicts, resistance emerges. This resistance is not laziness or lack of motivation; it is the mind protecting internal consistency. As a result, attempting to change behavior without addressing identity often leads to short-term success followed by relapse.

Reinventing identity begins with recognizing that identity is constructed, not fixed. It is formed through accumulated experiences, interpretations, and repeated behaviors. Each action provides evidence that either reinforces or challenges the existing self-concept. Over time, these interpretations solidify into identity statements such as "I am disciplined," "I avoid conflict," or "I struggle with consistency." These statements guide future behavior by setting expectations about what is possible or likely.

Change becomes possible when identity is treated as a dynamic system rather than a permanent label. This shift allows individuals to move from defending who they have been to intentionally shaping who they are becoming. The focus moves from outcome-based goals to identity-based alignment. Instead of asking, "What do I want to achieve?" the question becomes, "Who do I want to become, and how would that person act?"

Small, consistent behaviors play a crucial role in identity reinvention. The mind updates identity based on evidence, not intention. Large declarations without behavioral support are dismissed internally. In contrast, repeated small actions provide credible proof that a new identity is emerging. Each action serves as a data point, gradually reshaping belief about the self. Over time, what once felt forced begins to feel natural as identity adjusts to match behavior.

Interpretation of action is as important as action itself. When individuals consciously frame behavior as evidence of a chosen identity, the impact is amplified. For example, following through on a commitment can be interpreted as "I am becoming reliable," rather than as a single isolated success. This interpretive framing accelerates identity change by linking behavior directly to self-concept.

Emotional experience also shapes identity reinvention. Positive emotional feedback—such as pride, competence, or alignment—reinforces new identity narratives. When behavior is paired with emotional reward, the mind encodes it as meaningful. Conversely, excessive self-criticism weakens identity change by associating new behavior with emotional cost. Sustainable reinvention requires patience and emotional regulation, allowing the mind to adapt without threat.

Social context influences identity evolution as well. Feedback from others can either reinforce or challenge emerging self-concepts. Environments that support growth, experimentation, and authenticity reduce resistance to identity change. Conversely, environments that reinforce old labels slow reinvention. Selecting contexts that align with the desired identity increases consistency and confidence.

Importantly, reinventing identity does not require rejecting the past. Past behaviors and experiences are part of the learning process that produced the current self-concept. Reinvention involves reinterpreting those experiences rather than denying them. Previous limitations can be reframed as adaptations to earlier conditions rather than permanent traits. This reframing reduces internal conflict and allows identity to evolve without fragmentation.

Identity change is gradual and nonlinear. Old narratives may resurface under stress, and moments of inconsistency are expected. These moments do not negate progress; they provide information about where alignment is still developing. Persistence, rather than perfection, drives identity transformation.

Ultimately, behavior follows identity more reliably than motivation or willpower. When individuals reinvent identity intentionally, behavior shifts with less friction. Actions become expressions of who one is becoming rather than obligations imposed from outside. This alignment transforms change from a struggle into a process of integration, allowing behavior to stabilize and endure over time.

Chapter 10

Stress, Trauma, and Behavioral Responses

Stress and trauma exert a profound influence on human behavior, often shaping action in ways that feel automatic, disproportionate, or difficult to control. These influences are not signs of weakness or dysfunction; they are expressions of the mind's survival mechanisms responding to perceived threat. When stress becomes chronic or trauma remains unresolved, these mechanisms can dominate behavior long after the original danger has passed.

This chapter examines how the mind adapts to stress and trauma by prioritizing safety over growth. Under threat, psychological systems shift toward rapid response, emotional regulation, and threat avoidance. These adaptations are essential for survival, but they come at a cost. When the nervous system remains in a heightened state of alert, behavior becomes reactive rather than intentional. Decisions are guided by fear, vigilance, or withdrawal rather than reflective choice.

Trauma-based action patterns emerge when experiences overwhelm the individual's capacity to process them. The mind encodes these experiences emotionally, creating patterns designed to prevent recurrence. Avoidance, hypervigilance, emotional numbing, or compulsive control may develop as protective responses. While these patterns once served a purpose, they can restrict behavior and reduce flexibility in present circumstances.

The chapter also explores healing as a pathway to behavioral freedom. Healing does not involve erasing memory but integrating experience in a way that restores choice. As emotional charge diminishes and safety is reestablished, the mind regains its capacity for regulation and reflection. Behavior shifts from survival-driven reaction to intentional action.

By understanding stress and trauma as adaptive responses rather than personal flaws, individuals can approach change with compassion rather than self-judgment. This chapter lays the foundation for recognizing how healing expands behavioral possibility by restoring the balance between safety and growth.

Survival Mechanisms of the Mind

The human mind is fundamentally oriented toward survival. Long before conscious reasoning evaluates options, psychological systems scan for threat, predict danger, and prepare the body for action. These survival mechanisms evolved to protect against immediate physical harm, yet they continue to operate in modern environments where threats are often psychological rather than physical. Understanding these mechanisms is essential for explaining why behavior under stress can feel automatic, intense, and resistant to conscious control.

At the core of the survival response is the rapid detection of threat. The mind continuously evaluates internal and external signals, assessing whether a situation poses danger. This evaluation occurs beneath awareness and prioritizes speed over accuracy. When threat is perceived, the nervous system mobilizes energy for action. Attention narrows, physiological arousal increases, and behavior becomes focused on immediate safety rather than long-term planning.

Common survival responses include fight, flight, freeze, and fawn. Fight mobilizes confrontation and defense, flight promotes escape and avoidance, freeze results in immobility or dissociation, and fawn involves appeasement or compliance to reduce threat. These responses are not choices; they are automatic patterns activated when the mind perceives danger. Each response reflects an adaptive strategy that once increased the likelihood of survival in a specific context.

Survival mechanisms also influence perception and cognition. Under threat, the mind becomes hyper-focused on potential danger, amplifying negative information and suppressing nuance. Memory retrieval shifts toward threat-related experiences, reinforcing vigilance. This bias is adaptive in the short term but limiting when it persists. Decision-making becomes reactive, driven by urgency rather than reflection.

Stress activates survival mechanisms even in the absence of immediate danger. Chronic stress keeps the mind in a heightened state of alert, lowering the threshold for threat detection. In this state, minor challenges can trigger disproportionate responses. Behavior becomes governed by avoidance, control, or emotional reactivity as the mind attempts to manage perceived risk.

Importantly, survival mechanisms shape behavior beyond moments of crisis. Repeated activation conditions the mind to expect threat, embedding protective patterns into daily behavior. These patterns can include withdrawal from challenge, overworking to maintain control, emotional numbing to reduce pain, or hypervigilance in relationships. While these behaviors once served safety, they can restrict growth and connection when the original threat is no longer present.

Trauma intensifies survival responses by overwhelming the mind's capacity to process experience. When events exceed coping resources, survival mechanisms remain engaged to prevent recurrence. This ongoing activation can produce rigid behavioral patterns that feel compulsory rather than chosen. The mind prioritizes safety at all costs, often at the expense of flexibility and exploration.

Survival mechanisms are reinforced through emotional relief. When a behavior reduces anxiety or discomfort, it is reinforced as effective. Over time, the mind learns that certain responses reliably restore a sense of safety. This learning strengthens automaticity, making the behavior more likely to occur in similar contexts.

Understanding survival mechanisms reframes behavior that appears irrational or self-defeating. These behaviors are not failures of willpower; they are protective adaptations. Recognizing their function reduces self-blame and opens the possibility of change.

Change does not involve eliminating survival mechanisms but recalibrating them. Healing requires restoring a sense of safety so that the mind can disengage from constant defense. As safety increases, reflective processes regain influence, and behavior becomes more flexible.

Survival mechanisms of the mind reveal that behavior under stress is shaped by protection, not preference. By understanding these mechanisms, individuals can approach behavioral change with compassion, recognizing that safety must be addressed before growth can occur.

Trauma-Based Action Patterns

Trauma-based action patterns are behaviors shaped by experiences that overwhelmed an individual's ability to cope, process, or feel safe. These patterns are not conscious choices or personality traits; they are protective responses learned by the mind and body in moments of perceived danger. Once established, they persist as automatic strategies designed to prevent re-experiencing harm. Although these behaviors may appear irrational or self-sabotaging in the present, they are coherent when understood as survival adaptations.

Trauma alters how the mind interprets threat and safety. During overwhelming experiences, the nervous system shifts into survival mode, prioritizing immediate protection over reflection or learning. The brain encodes not only the event but also the emotional and physiological state associated with it. This encoding links certain cues—tones of voice, environments, relational dynamics, or internal sensations—with danger. When similar cues are encountered later, the trauma response is activated automatically, even if no real threat exists.

These automatic responses form trauma-based action patterns. Avoidance is one of the most common. Individuals may avoid situations, conversations, emotions, or responsibilities that unconsciously resemble past trauma. Avoidance reduces distress in the short term, reinforcing the behavior. Over time, it narrows life experience, limiting growth, connection, and opportunity.

Hypervigilance is another common pattern. The individual remains constantly alert for signs of threat, scanning environments and relationships for danger. This heightened awareness can lead to overinterpretation of neutral cues as threatening. Behavior becomes cautious, defensive, or controlling as the mind attempts to maintain safety. While hypervigilance once served survival, it often leads to chronic anxiety and exhaustion.

Some trauma-based patterns involve emotional numbing or detachment. When emotional pain was overwhelming, the mind may have learned to suppress feeling altogether. This strategy reduces distress but also reduces access to joy, motivation, and connection. Behavior may appear disengaged, indifferent, or unresponsive, masking an underlying protective mechanism rather than lack of care.

Compulsive control can also emerge from trauma. When past experiences involved unpredictability or helplessness, the mind may seek safety through control. This can manifest as perfectionism, rigidity, or excessive responsibility. These behaviors create an illusion of safety by reducing uncertainty, but they increase stress and limit flexibility.

Relational trauma often produces patterns centered on attachment. Some individuals may become excessively accommodating or people-pleasing to avoid conflict or abandonment. Others may withdraw emotionally or push others away to prevent vulnerability. These behaviors are not flaws; they are learned responses to relational threat.

Trauma-based patterns are maintained through emotional reinforcement. Each time a protective behavior reduces distress, the mind registers it as effective. This relief strengthens the pattern, making it more likely to activate in the future. Because the relief is immediate, the long-term costs are often overlooked by the nervous system.

Importantly, trauma-based action patterns operate beneath conscious awareness. Individuals may understand logically that a situation is safe yet still feel compelled to respond defensively. This disconnect can lead to self-criticism and confusion. Without understanding the trauma origin, individuals may blame themselves for behaviors that feel uncontrollable.

These patterns also influence identity. Repeated trauma responses can become integrated into self-concept, leading individuals to believe they are anxious, avoidant, or incapable. This identity reinforcement further stabilizes the pattern, making change feel threatening.

Healing trauma-based action patterns requires safety, not force. Logical reasoning alone cannot override survival responses. The nervous system must learn, through experience, that new contexts are safe. This learning occurs gradually through emotional regulation, supportive relationships, and repeated experiences that contradict threat expectations.

Awareness is a critical first step. Recognizing a behavior as trauma-based rather than character-based reduces shame and increases compassion. With awareness, individuals can begin to observe patterns without immediately acting on them, creating space for choice.

Trauma-based action patterns reveal the mind's commitment to protection. They persist because they once worked. When safety is restored and new emotional experiences are integrated, these patterns can soften. Behavior becomes less reactive and more intentional, allowing the individual to respond to the present rather than the past.

Understanding trauma-based action patterns transforms the narrative from "something is wrong with me" to "something happened to me." This shift is foundational for healing and for reclaiming behavioral freedom.

Healing as a Path to Behavioral Freedom

Behavioral freedom is often misunderstood as the ability to act without constraint or discomfort. In reality, true freedom emerges when individuals regain the capacity to choose how they respond rather than being driven by automatic survival patterns. For those shaped by stress and trauma, this freedom does not come from willpower or discipline alone; it comes through healing. Healing restores safety to the nervous system, allowing behavior to shift from reactive defense to intentional action.

When trauma remains unresolved, the mind prioritizes protection above all else. Survival mechanisms dominate behavior, narrowing options and reducing flexibility. In this state, actions are guided by fear, avoidance, or control rather than values or purpose. Healing addresses this imbalance by reducing the emotional charge associated with past experiences, enabling the nervous system to distinguish between past threat and present reality.

Healing begins with safety. The nervous system must perceive that danger has passed before it can relax its grip on protective behavior. This safety is both internal and external. Internally, it involves developing the capacity to regulate emotion and tolerate discomfort without immediate escape. Externally, it involves environments and relationships that provide consistency, validation, and support. Without safety, attempts at change trigger further defense.

Awareness is a foundational element of healing. By recognizing how past experiences shape current behavior, individuals can separate identity from adaptation. Behaviors once viewed as flaws are reframed as survival strategies. This reframing reduces shame and self-judgment, which themselves perpetuate stress responses. Compassion creates space for regulation and reflection.

Emotional processing is central to healing. Trauma is not stored as narrative memory alone but as emotional and physiological patterns. Healing involves allowing previously avoided emotions to be experienced in manageable ways. This exposure updates the nervous system's expectations, teaching it that emotion can be tolerated without danger. As emotional tolerance increases, the urgency of protective behaviors decreases.

Behavioral freedom also requires integration of new experiences. When individuals act differently and experience safety rather than harm, the mind revises its predictions. Each safe experience weakens trauma-based associations and strengthens alternative responses. This learning is gradual and repetitive, reflecting how the original patterns were formed.

Self-regulation skills support this process. Practices that calm the nervous system—such as grounding, pacing, and emotional labeling—reduce reactivity and increase choice. These skills do not eliminate emotional response but prevent it from overwhelming decision-making. With regulation, reflective processes regain influence.

Healing also involves redefining identity. Trauma-based behaviors often become integrated into self-concept. As healing progresses, individuals can begin to see themselves not as broken, but as adaptive and capable of growth. This identity shift supports new behavior by aligning action with a renewed sense of self.

Importantly, healing is not linear. Old patterns may resurface under stress, and setbacks are part of the process. These moments are not failures but indicators of where safety is still developing. Patience and persistence are essential.

Healing as a path to behavioral freedom emphasizes restoration rather than correction. It recognizes that behavior shaped by trauma is not wrong; it is protective. By addressing the underlying need for safety, individuals regain access to choice. Behavior becomes guided by present goals and values rather than past threat.

Ultimately, healing expands the range of possible action. As survival responses soften, individuals can engage more fully with life, take risks aligned with purpose, and respond flexibly to challenge. Behavioral freedom emerges not from eliminating fear, but from restoring the capacity to act despite it—with awareness, choice, and intention.

Chapter 11

Willpower, Discipline, and Psychological Energy

Willpower is often portrayed as the ultimate solution to behavioral change—a personal resource that, if strengthened, can overcome distraction, temptation, and inconsistency. Discipline is similarly framed as a matter of character: those who succeed are assumed to possess more of it. While willpower and discipline do play important roles in guiding behavior, this perspective is incomplete. It overlooks the psychological and energetic limits that govern self-control and explains why effort alone so often fails.

This chapter examines willpower not as an unlimited trait, but as a finite psychological resource influenced by emotional state, cognitive load, and environmental demand. Self-control requires mental energy. Each act of regulation—resisting impulse, making decisions, managing emotion—draws from the same limited pool. When this energy is depleted, discipline weakens, and behavior becomes reactive rather than intentional. This depletion explains why people often make sound decisions early in the day and struggle later, despite unchanged intentions.

Mental fatigue plays a central role in decision collapse. As cognitive resources are exhausted, the mind defaults to familiar, low-effort behaviors. Habits, emotional impulses, and environmental cues gain influence, while reflective judgment loses strength. This shift is not a moral failure; it is a predictable response to cognitive strain.

The chapter also challenges the idea that sustainable self-control depends on constant effort. Lasting discipline emerges not from relentless willpower, but from systems that conserve psychological energy. By designing habits, environments, and identities that reduce the need for active control, individuals can act consistently without relying on moment-to-moment restraint.

Understanding the limits of willpower reframes discipline as a strategic process rather than a test of endurance. This chapter lays the foundation for building self-control that is resilient, humane, and aligned with how the mind actually functions.

The Limits of Willpower

Willpower is often treated as a personal reservoir of strength—something that can be summoned at will to overcome temptation, distraction, and resistance. In reality, willpower is a limited psychological resource that fluctuates depending on emotional state, cognitive load, and context. Understanding its limits is essential for explaining why people can act with discipline in some moments and struggle profoundly in others, despite unchanged intentions.

At a cognitive level, willpower relies on executive functions such as attention, inhibition, and working memory. These functions allow individuals to suppress impulses, hold goals in mind, and choose actions aligned with long-term outcomes. However, these functions are metabolically and psychologically costly. They require mental energy, focus, and emotional regulation. As a result, willpower cannot be applied continuously without consequence.

One of the most common misconceptions about willpower is that failure indicates weakness of character. This belief leads individuals to blame themselves when self-control lapses, rather than examining the conditions under which the lapse occurred. In reality, willpower fails predictably under specific circumstances: stress, fatigue, emotional overload, decision density, and environmental pressure. These factors reduce the brain's capacity to regulate behavior, regardless of personal values or intelligence.

Willpower is also context-dependent. A person may display remarkable discipline in one domain and struggle in another. This inconsistency is not hypocrisy; it reflects varying demands on psychological energy. Situations that are emotionally charged or cognitively complex consume more regulatory capacity, leaving less available for impulse control. Over time, repeated demands without recovery exhaust willpower reserves.

Another limitation of willpower lies in its reactive nature. Willpower is often deployed after temptation arises, requiring the individual to actively resist. This constant resistance creates psychological friction. The more frequently willpower is used as a defense against impulse, the more quickly it is depleted. This dynamic explains why relying solely on willpower produces short bursts of discipline followed by collapse.

Importantly, willpower does not operate in isolation. It competes with emotional urgency, habit strength, and environmental cues. When these opposing forces are strong, willpower must work harder to assert control. In such cases, even strong intentions can be overwhelmed. This does not mean willpower is useless; it means it is insufficient as a standalone strategy.

Understanding the limits of willpower shifts the focus from endurance to design. Instead of asking how to become stronger, the more effective question is how to reduce reliance on willpower altogether. When behavior is structured to require less active control, consistency improves naturally.

Willpower is best understood as a short-term stabilizer rather than a long-term solution. It is useful for initiating change or navigating unexpected challenges, but it cannot sustain behavior indefinitely. Sustainable action emerges when systems, habits, and identity reduce the need for constant regulation.

Recognizing the limits of willpower is not discouraging; it is liberating. It allows individuals to stop fighting their own psychology and begin working with it. When willpower is respected as a finite resource, behavior change becomes more strategic, compassionate, and effective.

Mental Fatigue and Decision Collapse

Mental fatigue is one of the most underestimated forces shaping human behavior. It refers not simply to feeling tired, but to the depletion of cognitive and emotional resources required for decision-making and self-regulation. When mental fatigue sets in, the mind's ability to evaluate options, manage emotion, and resist impulse diminishes. The result is decision collapse—a state in which behavior defaults to habit, impulse, or avoidance rather than intention.

Every decision carries a cognitive cost. Evaluating options, weighing consequences, and exercising restraint all draw from the same pool of psychological energy. In modern environments filled with constant choices, interruptions, and demands, this energy is consumed rapidly. As mental fatigue accumulates, the brain seeks efficiency by reducing effortful processing. Reflective judgment weakens, and automatic responses take over.

Decision collapse does not occur suddenly; it unfolds gradually. Early signs include reduced patience, increased irritability, and difficulty concentrating. As fatigue deepens, decisions become more impulsive, rigid, or avoidant. The mind favors familiar behaviors because they require less cognitive effort. This explains why individuals often revert to old habits at the end of the day, even after making progress earlier.

Stress accelerates mental fatigue by increasing emotional load. When the nervous system is activated, more resources are diverted toward managing perceived threat. This leaves fewer resources available for self-control and reasoning. Under chronic stress, decision collapse can become a persistent state, making intentional behavior difficult to sustain.

Mental fatigue also explains inconsistency in values-based behavior. Individuals may sincerely endorse certain principles yet violate them under exhaustion. This discrepancy is not hypocrisy; it reflects reduced access to reflective processes. The values still exist, but the capacity to act on them is temporarily impaired.

Importantly, decision collapse is predictable and preventable. It is not a personal failing but a signal that cognitive demand has exceeded capacity. Without this understanding, individuals often respond to collapse with self-criticism, which increases stress and further depletes resources.

Recovery is essential. Rest, emotional regulation, and reduction of decision load restore cognitive capacity. Simplifying choices, creating routines, and automating decisions conserve energy and reduce the likelihood of collapse. When fewer decisions require active regulation, the mind remains more resilient.

Awareness of mental fatigue allows individuals to plan strategically. High-stakes decisions can be scheduled when energy is highest. Low-energy periods can be reserved for routine tasks. This alignment improves consistency without requiring greater effort.

Decision collapse reveals that behavior is deeply tied to energy management. When energy is respected, judgment remains accessible. When it is ignored, collapse is inevitable. Understanding this dynamic is crucial for building systems that support intentional action rather than undermining it.

Building Sustainable Self-Control

Sustainable self-control is not the result of constant restraint or extraordinary discipline. It emerges from systems that align behavior with psychological capacity. Rather than relying on moment-to-moment willpower, sustainable self-control reduces friction, conserves energy, and supports intentional action through structure and design.

The first principle of sustainable self-control is reducing unnecessary demand. When behavior requires frequent inhibition, it becomes fragile. Effective self-control minimizes exposure to triggers and simplifies decision-making. By designing environments that support desired behavior, individuals reduce reliance on active regulation.

Habit formation is central to sustainability. Habits shift behavior from effortful control to automatic execution. Once a behavior is habitual, it no longer consumes significant self-regulatory resources. Building habits requires consistency and repetition, but once established, they free cognitive energy for other tasks.

Identity alignment further strengthens self-control. When behavior is seen as an expression of identity rather than an obligation, resistance decreases. Actions feel internally motivated rather than externally imposed. This alignment reduces the emotional cost of regulation and increases persistence.

Emotional regulation is another critical component. Many lapses in self-control occur not because of temptation, but because of unmanaged emotion. Developing the ability to tolerate discomfort, frustration, or boredom reduces the need for impulsive relief. This capacity allows individuals to pause and choose rather than react.

Energy management supports self-control over time. Adequate rest, nutrition, and recovery restore cognitive capacity. Sustainable self-control accounts for human limits rather than denying them. It plans for fluctuation rather than assuming constant strength.

Systems outperform intentions. Clear routines, predefined rules, and environmental cues guide behavior automatically. When the system is well-designed, behavior follows with minimal effort. Self-control becomes embedded in structure rather than enforced through constant vigilance.

Importantly, sustainable self-control is flexible, not rigid. It allows for adaptation and recovery rather than perfection. Lapses are treated as information rather than failure, guiding refinement of systems and supports.

Building sustainable self-control requires shifting perspective. The question is not "How can I try harder?" but "How can I make this easier to do consistently?" This shift transforms self-control from a battle into a design challenge.

When self-control is sustainable, behavior becomes reliable without being exhausting. Action aligns with intention not because of force, but because the system supports it. This is the foundation of long-term consistency and psychological resilience.

Chapter 12

Conscious Awareness and Intentional Action

Throughout this book, we have examined the hidden psychological forces that shape human behavior—forces that operate beneath awareness and influence action automatically. This final chapter brings those insights together by focusing on the role of conscious awareness as the gateway to intentional action. Awareness does not eliminate impulses, emotions, habits, or social influence. Instead, it creates the space in which choice becomes possible.

Conscious awareness is the ability to observe thoughts, emotions, bodily sensations, and behavioral urges without immediately reacting to them. This capacity transforms experience from something that happens to the individual into something that can be examined and guided. When awareness is absent, behavior is governed by automatic patterns formed through conditioning, habit, and survival responses. When awareness is present, these patterns can be interrupted.

This chapter explores how psychological self-awareness develops and why it is essential for behavioral change. Awareness allows individuals to recognize triggers, emotional shifts, and habitual responses in real time. This recognition weakens automaticity by inserting a moment of pause between stimulus and response. In that pause, intention can be reasserted.

The chapter also examines how intentional action differs from reactive behavior. Intentional action is guided by values, meaning, and long-term purpose rather than immediate emotion or external pressure. Designing action intentionally involves aligning behavior with identity and goals, while accounting for human limitations and psychological reality.

Conscious awareness is not a passive state; it is an active skill that can be strengthened through practice. As awareness deepens, behavior becomes more flexible and less driven by unconscious patterns. This chapter serves as both a conclusion and a transition—showing how awareness integrates all previous themes and offers a practical path toward acting with clarity, agency, and purpose.

Developing Psychological Self-Awareness

Psychological self-awareness is the capacity to observe one's internal experience—thoughts, emotions, bodily sensations, and impulses—without immediately identifying with or acting on them. It is not self-criticism or constant introspection; it is a skill that allows individuals to notice what is happening internally as it happens. This awareness forms the foundation of intentional behavior because action cannot be consciously guided if the forces driving it remain unseen.

Most behavior operates on autopilot. Thoughts arise, emotions follow, and actions occur in rapid sequence, often without conscious evaluation. Psychological self-awareness interrupts this chain by bringing attention to the process itself. Instead of being immersed in thought or emotion, the individual becomes an observer of it. This shift creates distance, reducing the automatic influence of internal states on behavior.

Self-awareness develops through attention and reflection. Attention involves noticing internal signals as they arise—tension in the body, shifts in emotion, recurring thoughts, or impulses toward action. Reflection involves recognizing patterns across time, such as consistent emotional triggers or habitual responses. Together, these processes reveal how internal dynamics shape behavior.

Emotional awareness is a critical component. Many actions are driven by unrecognized emotional states rather than conscious choice. When emotions remain unnamed, they exert greater control. Identifying emotions—such as anxiety, frustration, or desire—reduces their intensity and increases regulatory capacity. This naming process transforms emotion from a driver into information.

Cognitive awareness also plays a role. Thoughts often present themselves as facts rather than interpretations. Psychological self-awareness involves recognizing thoughts as mental events rather than objective reality. This recognition weakens their authority and allows alternative perspectives to emerge. When thoughts are observed rather than obeyed, behavior becomes more flexible.

Bodily awareness is equally important. The body often signals stress, fear, or excitement before the mind articulates it. Tightness, restlessness, or changes in breathing provide early indicators of internal state. Attuning to these signals increases responsiveness and prevents escalation into reactive behavior.

Developing self-awareness requires practice, particularly during low-stress moments. Under pressure, awareness narrows. Regular reflection strengthens the capacity to remain aware even when emotions intensify. This practice does not eliminate emotional response; it enhances the ability to remain present within it.

Importantly, self-awareness is nonjudgmental. Judgment increases defensiveness and resistance, reducing awareness. Observing internal experience with curiosity and neutrality allows patterns to surface without triggering avoidance or self-criticism.

Psychological self-awareness empowers choice by revealing the forces influencing action. When these forces are seen clearly, they lose their invisibility and dominance. Awareness does not guarantee perfect behavior, but it provides the necessary condition for intentional action. Without it, behavior remains governed by unseen patterns. With it, action becomes a matter of choice rather than reflex.

Interrupting Automatic Behavior

Automatic behavior arises from habits, emotional conditioning, and learned responses designed to conserve energy and manage experience efficiently. While these behaviors are often useful, they become limiting when they operate without awareness or flexibility. Interrupting automatic behavior does not mean eliminating habits; it means regaining the capacity to choose when and how they operate.

Automatic behavior follows a predictable sequence: a trigger activates an internal state, which leads to a habitual response. This sequence occurs rapidly, often bypassing conscious evaluation. Interruption requires identifying and intervening within this sequence. Awareness is the entry point. Without recognizing that a pattern is active, interruption is impossible.

The most effective interruption occurs at the moment of activation. Early signals—emotional shifts, bodily sensations, or familiar thoughts—indicate that an automatic response is forming. Recognizing these signals creates a brief pause. This pause is not about suppression; it is about delaying action long enough for conscious evaluation to occur.

Pausing is a powerful regulatory tool. Even a short delay allows emotional intensity to subside and reflective processes to re-engage. During this pause, individuals can ask simple questions: What is driving this urge? What outcome does this behavior usually produce? Is there an alternative response? These questions redirect attention from impulse to intention.

Interrupting automatic behavior also involves reducing reinforcement. Automatic behaviors persist because they provide some form of relief or reward. Identifying the payoff clarifies why the behavior exists. When alternative behaviors provide similar relief without long-term cost, the automatic pattern weakens.

Environment plays a critical role in interruption. Automatic behaviors are cue-dependent. Changing cues—physical, social, or temporal—reduces activation. Removing triggers or altering routines lowers the frequency of automatic responses, making interruption more accessible.

Importantly, interruption is not about control through force. Forcing suppression often increases rebound behavior. Effective interruption is based on redirection rather than resistance. The goal is to shift response, not to deny experience.

Practice strengthens interruption capacity. Each successful pause reinforces awareness and weakens automaticity. Over time, the mind learns that immediate reaction is not required. This learning increases behavioral flexibility.

Interrupting automatic behavior is a skill developed through repetition and patience. It does not eliminate habit instantly, but it restores choice. With consistent interruption, behavior becomes less reflexive and more responsive to intention, values, and context.

Designing Actions With Purpose

Intentional action is not simply choosing a goal and applying effort. It involves designing behavior that aligns with values, identity, and psychological reality. Purpose-driven action accounts for human limitations, emotional dynamics, and environmental influence. When actions are designed rather than forced, consistency and meaning increase.

Purpose begins with clarity. Purposeful action is guided by values—principles that provide direction beyond immediate outcomes. Values clarify why action matters, sustaining motivation when discomfort arises. Without this connection, action becomes fragile, relying on willpower alone.

Designing action with purpose involves translating values into behavior. This translation requires specificity. Vague intentions produce inconsistent action. Clear, concrete behaviors provide structure and reduce cognitive demand. Purposeful design turns abstract meaning into actionable steps.

Alignment with identity strengthens purpose. When actions are framed as expressions of who one is becoming, resistance decreases. Identity-based design shifts motivation from obligation to self-expression. Behavior becomes internally motivated rather than externally imposed.

Simplicity is central to purposeful design. Overly complex plans increase cognitive load and reduce follow through. Purposeful actions are realistic, repeatable, and scalable. Small actions performed consistently carry more impact than ambitious plans rarely executed.

Environment is part of design. Purposeful behavior is supported by cues, routines, and structures that reduce reliance on willpower. Designing surroundings to support desired action makes consistency easier and more reliable.

Feedback loops reinforce purpose. Tracking progress and reflecting on impact maintain engagement. Purpose deepens when individuals see how actions align with values and produce meaningful outcomes.

Purposeful design also includes flexibility. Rigid plans break under stress.

Adaptive design allows adjustment without abandoning direction. This flexibility preserves purpose even when conditions change.

Designing actions with purpose transforms behavior from reaction to expression. Action becomes a reflection of values rather than a response to impulse. Over time, this alignment creates a sense of coherence and agency, allowing individuals to act intentionally in a complex and demanding world.

Purposeful action is not about perfection. It is about alignment. When behavior is designed with awareness, identity, and values in mind, consistency becomes more natural, and action becomes meaningful rather than forced.

www.ingramcontent.com/pod-product-compliance
Lightning Source LLC
LaVergne TN
LVHW050922210926
848482LV00012B/496

* 9 7 8 9 6 9 9 7 9 7 1 3 2 *